Women on Campus

The Unfinished Liberation
Women on Campus

Edited by
George W. Bonham

With an introduction by Elizabeth Janeway

Routledge
Taylor & Francis Group

LONDON AND NEW YORK

Originally published in 1975 by *Change*

Published 2006 by Transaction Publishers

Published 2017 by Routledge
2 Park Square, Milton Park, Abingdon, Oxon OX14 4RN
711 Third Avenue, New York, NY 10017, USA

Routledge is an imprint of the Taylor & Francis Group, an informa business

Copyright © 2006 by Taylor & Francis.

All rights reserved. No part of this book may be reprinted or reproduced or utilised in any form or by any electronic, mechanical, or other means, now known or hereafter invented, including photocopying and recording, or in any information storage or retrieval system, without permission in writing from the publishers.

Notice:
Product or corporate names may be trademarks or registered trademarks, and are used only for identification and explanation without intent to infringe.

Library of Congress Catalog Number: 2005053878

Library of Congress Cataloging-in-Publication Data

Women on campus : the unfinished liberation / George W. Bonham, editor ; with an introduction by Elizabeth Janeway.
   p. cm.
  Originally published: New Rochelle, N.Y. : Change, 1975. With new introd.
  ISBN 1-4128-0559-7 (pbk. : alk. paper)
   1. Sex discrimination in higher education—United States. 2. Women—Education (Higher)—United States. I. Bonham, George W., 1925-

LC212.862.W665   2006
378.1'982—dc22   2005053878

ISBN 13: 978-1-4128-0559-9 (pbk)

Contents

George W. Bonham: Foreword ... 8
Elizabeth Janeway: Women on Campus: The Unfinished Liberation ... 10

The Odds Against

Ruth R. Hawkins: The Odds Against Women ... 28
Donna Martin: The Wives of Academe ... 34
Angela Stent: The Rhodes: Still Blocked ... 44
Charles J. Sugnet: The Uncertain Progress of Affirmative Action ... 53

Fighting the Odds

Catharine R. Stimpson: The New Feminism and Women's Studies ... 69
Virginia Barber: The Women's Revolt in the MLA ... 85
Bari Watkins: Women and History ... 95
Jean Collins: The Feminist Press ... 102
Easy Klein: Make Policy, Not Coffee ... 110
Cynthia Secor: Lesbians—The Doors Open ... 116

The Personal Voice

Celia Morris: Learning the Hard Way ... 125
Elaine B. Hopkins: Unemployed! an Academic Woman's Saga ... 140

Women with Impact

Elizabeth Tidball: The Search for Talented Women ... 152
Ruth Fischer: Black, Female—and Qualified ... 160
Nina McCain: Jacquelyn Mattfeld of Brown ... 167

At the Seven Sisters

Catharine R. Stimpson: Women at Bryn Mawr   174
Kate Millett: Women and War   195
Caroline Bird: Women's Lib and the Women's Colleges   220

Back to College

Pat Durchholz and Janet O'Connor: Why Women Go Back to College   236
Elisabeth Hansot: A "Second-Chance" Program for Women   242
Diane Rothbard Margolis: A Fair Return   249

Illustrations: p. 47, Joan Schum; p. 114, James Flora; pp. 43, 109, 124, 139, 151, 159, 173, 235, 248, Rick Schreiter.

About the Authors

Virginia Barber, a literary agent, is coauthor, along with Merrill Skaggs, of a book on motherhood to be published by Bobbs-Merrill in 1975.

Caroline Bird is a frequent lecturer on the status of women. She is the author of *Born Female, Everything A Woman Needs to Know to Get Paid What She's Worth*, and *The Case Against College* (1975), all published by David McKay.

Jean Collins is a New York-based journalist specializing in education and medicine.

Pat Durchholz, a graduate student in business administration, is the Ford administrative intern in the president's office of the University of Cincinnati.

Ruth Fischer, associate editor of *Change*, formerly was an editor for the Associated Press. Her articles, essays, and reviews have appeared in *Change, The New Republic, The Nation, Playboy, Consumer Reports* and *Money*.

Elisabeth Hansot works at the National Institute of Education. She was a contributor to the HEW report *Work in America*, and the author of *Perfection and Progress: Two Modes of Utopian Thought*, published by the Massachusetts Institute of Technology Press.

Ruth R. Hawkins is social science editor with the Educational Development Corporation in Palo Alto, California. She has taught at Purdue and Fordham, and is a member of the National Organization for Women (NOW).

Elaine B. Hopkins is a doctoral candidate at the University of Texas. Her sex discrimination complaint against Western Illinois University is pending with the Illinois Fair Employment Practices Commission.

Elizabeth Janeway is past president of the Authors Guild. She is a member of the Barnard College Board of Trustees, a director of the MacDowell Colony, and a member of the executive board of PEN, the international writers' organization. She is the author of *Man's World, Woman's Place*. Her latest book is *Between Myth and Morning: Women Awakening*, published by William Morrow.

Easy Klein is an educational filmmaker and a free-lance writer who contributes frequently to *Change*.

Diane Rothbard Margolis is writing her doctoral dissertation and preparing a study on women in political organizations under a grant from the Center for the American Woman and Politics at Rutgers University.

Donna Martin is managing editor of the publishing company Sheed and Ward, in Mission, Kansas. Her free-lance articles on education and publishing have appeared in *Publishers Weekly*, *Scholarly Publishing*, *Kanava* (in Helsinki), and *Change*.

Nina McCain is a Sunday feature writer and former education editor of the *Boston Globe*. She is a frequent contributor to *Change*.

Kate Millett is the author of the well-known *Sexual Politics* and *Flying*.

Celia Morris is senior editor of *Change*. Her writing has appeared in *Change*, *Mosaic*, the *Texas Observer*, and the *Colby Library Quarterly*.

Janet O'Connor, a graduate student in sociology, is assistant director of alumni affairs at the University of Cincinnati.

Cynthia Secor is a free-lance writer and co-chairperson of the Modern Language Association Commission on the Status of Women in the Profession.

Angela Stent, a teaching fellow in the government department at Harvard, has a special interest in the problems of women's education. She is a free-lance writer and a correspondent for the *London Times Higher Education Supplement*.

Catharine R. Stimpson, an assistant professor of English at Barnard, edited two editions of congressional hearings on sex discrimination. A regular contributor to *Change*, she also has written for *The Nation* and *Ms*.

Charles J. Sugnet teaches English at the University of Minnesota.

Elizabeth Tidball, professor of physiology at the George Washington University Medical Center in Washington, D.C., frequently speaks before college and professional groups on the education and professional development of women.

Bari Watkins, a graduate student at Yale, is completing a dissertation called "American Academic Social Theory and Labor Reform, 1883-1915."

Foreword

It is almost one hundred years since Ibsen brought Nora out of her doll's house, a relative heartbeat of history, but an agonizing eternity for those interred in their places by sexual stereotyping and the panegyrical celebration of *Kinder*, *Küche*, and *Kirche*.

The frustrations of talented women academics unable to find their fair share of places in a profession largely male-dominated and currently in the throes of fiscal and ideological impoverishment may overshadow the profound gains that will inevitably follow their present efforts. The latter are crucial, of course, but in the long term perhaps less pivotal than a new open-mindedness in scholarship that will emerge through wider participation of women scholars in the intellectual and cultural affairs of the nation.

While in fact the immediate victories of academic women may seem sparse in terms of their expectations, the long-range consequences are likely to be far more profound and salutary. A glance backward illustrates the point. Toward the end of the last century some of our best colleges helped lay the groundwork for the present feminist movement, though it is doubtful that they were fully conscious of their historic roles. In the 1880s Bryn Mawr, Oberlin, Smith, and Cornell, among others, produced a remarkable group of first-generation women college graduates who went on to create a tradition of women's involvement in the affairs of their time. Women such as Jane Addams, Mary Simkowitch, Lillian Wald, and Mary McDowell came to their social convictions largely through the experiences of their college days. A thousand later struggles were built on their early and often frustrating work.

Academic life now tends to be more polite and theoretically more liberal. But under even the best circumstances, some academics have been trained since their graduate days in intellectual condescension. One tends to agree with the frequent charge of feminists that preconceptions and unexamined assumptions run rampant in education. When one woman historian was charged with not presenting "the other side," she quipped that "the other side is all around us." Perhaps so, but it is by no means a hopeless picture.

While statistics on women's entry into academia are not yet encouraging, there have been some significant advances that will permanently change the tone and fiber of the academy. Spurred on by three major pieces of federal legislation, educational leaders and their institutions have had their collective consciousness raised to the point where equal opportunities for both sexes now get a healthy airing.

When Congresswoman Edith Green of Oregon held the first congressional hearings on sex discrimination in education in June 1970, not a single representative from the Washington educational establishment testified. There is no sex discrimination on campus, it was said, and there is no problem. Half a decade later, the problem that was no problem is a major topic of concern.

Here and there, women now hold important academic posts, and to the academy's Old Boys' network will soon be added an Old Girls' network. Still, as Bernice Sandler of the Association of American Colleges is fond of saying, the best chance for a woman to become a college president is through the nunnery.

More significantly, academic women no longer show as much anxiety about coming across as the intellectual equals or superiors of men. Women are beginning to play significant new roles in the academic community, and they are opening minds and hearts to new human possibilities.

—*George W. Bonham*
Editor, *Change* Magazine

Women on Campus: The Unfinished Liberation

By Elizabeth Janeway

Women on Campus: The Unfinished Liberation! If you want a measure of the social change of our times, join me for a moment in speculating on what that title would have suggested a scant 20 years ago, when presidents of women's colleges were peering into the clouded crystal ball of the fifties in the hope of discovering a cure for the strange malaise which was overtaking the brightest and best of their alumnae. "What am I doing here?" graduates of the Seven Sisters were asking themselves as they sorted the laundry or put the vacuum cleaner together to give the venetian blinds a thorough going-over. Perhaps even more often the question was, "What was I doing there—listening to lectures on Seventeenth Century French Poetry, Organic Chemistry, and Money and Banking—when I was fated by the Destiny of Anatomy to end up here?" For the decade of the fifties was not one in which the graduates of even the most prestigious women's colleges easily contemplated a change in their fate, their status, or their occupation. Married they must aspire to be, housewives they must expect to become.

What that meant is thoroughly documented. To

take an accessible source, in June of 1949 the *New York Times* published a survey of responses to a questionnaire sent by the Seven Sister colleges to graduates of the class of 1934. Eighty-two percent of my classmates (as they were until the Great Depression constrained me to become a premature drop-out) reported that they were married, "and happily too." At least, less than 7 percent had been divorced and half of those had remarried. Eighty-eight percent of the married graduates had children; in 1949, the unmarried presumably were not asked. "Socially, life for '34 revolves around the home, the bridge table, and her clubs," the *Times* reported, though it did mention replies from a few "individualists," one of whom "gets most pleasure from telephoning, one from television, and three from drinking."

And what did our alumnae think of their education? Well, almost all of them would have gone to college again, though only 30 percent were certain that they were going to send their daughters. Nonetheless, one in five was critical enough of her college experience to feel that changes should be made. "College," they said over and over, "prepared me for something I'm not: to be a professor, and not for the life I lead; for something better than the monotonies of dusting, sweeping, cooking, and mending." And what was the remedy proposed? To change—not the world—but the curriculum. "More practical training...courses in cooking, dressmaking, household management, child care, and psychology, even in entertaining and 'how to have a dinner party,' are among the suggestions."

Let us not think that such a program of women's studies was anathema to educators. The retiring head of Wellesley, addressing herself to this group of alumnae, declared, "College failed to teach these women that most people accomplish most in the world by working through established social institutions, and that the family is entirely respectable as a sphere of activity." A contemporary head of my own Seventh Sister was convinced that women's education should not parallel that of men, but relate to their expected future lives, which meant an expected career as a housewife. As for any other possible career, it was conceived as being a stop-gap between graduation and marriage, or a kind of insurance against the bad luck of spinsterhood. George Schuster, president of Hunter College, declared in 1952, "The country wants young ladies who can graduate from college, can type, spell, and take a job as a secretary." In 1956 a *New York Times* story on Radcliffe women holding doctorates was headlined, "Even a PhD Can't Escape the Kitchen." And in 1957, David Riesman reportedly offered the American Association of University Women his condolences on the fact that "in spite of 'good statistical evidence' that women can earn their degrees and still find a husband, a third or more drop out after the freshman year. The social scientist expressed confidence that an education could be given women that would prepare them for the highest and best eventualities of marriage and career."

Please do not imagine that this brief historical review is intended to evoke an attack of the Virginia Slims Syndrome: "We've come a long way, Baby, and so we can stop right here and relax." On the contrary, the evidence that we have made some progress suggests to me that we should redouble our efforts, for once The Old Ark's A-Movering, it's wise to keep on pushing. I do think, however, that we are entitled to take some cheer from the evidence cited above of how entirely wrong-headed were the agitations of the fifties; for if academic respectability was arrantly mistaken two decades ago, it may be just as off-base today, its assumptions as false, its conclusions as dotty. To take an example to hand: the idea that affirmative action to increase employment of women and minority members will somehow subvert an existing process, by which promotion and tenure are now granted on the grounds of merit, is patently ridiculous. Academia has been getting on without half the research talent and teaching skill it might have laid claim to just by ignoring women. Add in the overlooked male half of the minorities, and the store of neglected merit and ability climbs still further. How the Establishment can suppose that restricting its talent pool to 30 or 40 percent of the population should be labelled "a search for excellence" or "promotion for merit" is—well, beyond me. The Elite has its reasons, shall we say, that Reason knows not of.

No, I have offered my bit of history from the fifties not in order to justify appeasement, but rather to reassure those who are worried about disagreeing with today's learned men on today's issues. Many of these sages were happily, convincedly wrong 20 years ago, just as wrong as any human being (always including ourselves) may be. They turned their analytic and sapient gaze on the world and perceived that the education given women "did not prepare them for life." Clearly, then, this education had to be changed or women's lives would be swamped and flooded by frustration and anger. And while they pondered this deep question, women's lives started to change. The alteration picked up speed, frustration and anger supplying the motivation for women to meet the challenges of reality and cope with the world which was demanding that they find economically valuable work which would engage their capabilities—and in the twinkling of an eye, all that fuss about how to educate our daughters blew out of our minds, and vanished in thin air. Women's education has ceased to mean "cooking, dressmaking, household management, child care, and entertaining," and now denotes the wide range of topics discussed in the collection of articles from *Change* Magazine grouped together here.

I repeat, the progress we have made does not mean that we have reached our goals, nor even an acceptable place for a rest-halt. Equality of opportunity on campus is still a hopeful dream. But the stock taking which these articles offer us is a valuable enterprise. Not only does it indicate those areas where advance has taken place—or not taken place. It also directs our attention to some problems, and some possibilities, which are frequently overlooked in discussions of the obvious issues. Let's look at a few. That there is opposition to the promotion of women among older male professors is a commonplace. Back in 1969, when affirmative action programs were still sleeping underground, Ruth Hawkins described "The Odds Against Women." It is an interesting and still useful report of the actual situation; but its analysis of the psychological background to the situation is even more telling.

Thus, says Hawkins, the male Mandarinate of Academia prefers to teach graduate rather than undergraduate students. It rates research above teaching in its hierarchy of values. And it uses, as its measure of accomplishment, the record of publication of aspirant faculty members. Any academic who questions this complex of attitudes and beliefs is clearly at a disadvantage in seeking to rise in her/his profession. Members of both sexes question the complex; but women, feminist women most of all, question these values with special seriousness. No doubt this questioning is based in part on experience. Women publish less than men, having less time to write and to research, since they habitually add the job of housekeeping to that of professor. In the past they have been steered toward teaching rather than research, and to teaching at the undergraduate level. But experience is not the only reason they question the traditional standards by which research, publication, and teaching of candidates for higher degrees are assumed to be the most valuable occupation in the university. The broadening base of the student body, and the increasing need for teaching which is involved and responsive, require rather different standards, standards which are more flexibly adaptable to changing conditions on campus. These changes in themselves validate the challenge which women have mounted to the traditional professorial icon.

Elaine Hopkins' report on her years of wrestling with the red tape of departmental standards and requirements for employment carries the story forward from 1969 to 1973. It is the same story of self-defeating rigidity. Hopkins, a competent teacher of undergraduate English courses, was recurrently threatened with dismissal from a Midwestern state university because she had not made "adequate progress" toward a doctorate. Fair enough, on the Old Boys' standard. But when Hopkins did find a good and stimulating doctoral program that emphasized the teaching of composition and literature at the undergraduate level, which was exactly what she was doing and apparently what her department needed done, it was disapproved on the stunning grounds that, once she got her doctorate, she would have nothing to teach! And why not? Because "everyone knows" that holders of PhDs don't want to teach literature and composition to undergraduates, they want to specialize, do research, and publish. "Having originated in the medieval monastery, the modern university is a world of credentialed scholars competing for status," writes Hopkins. I would like to modify her definition only slightly. That's what the educational Establishment *thinks* the university is, and will remain. Can they keep it so, in the face of a changing student body and changing social demands?

Other articles collected here pay special attention to one component of the changing student body which will certainly grow in importance and is already present in greater force than is realized by the Establishment. These are returning, or continuing students, women who are getting ready to enter the labor force as their children grow older (and inflation grows sharper), or middle-aged people, already working, who want to change or upgrade their careers. These women are the subject of two analyses included here, one personal and experiential, and one based on a statistical study; but some investigation of my own for a paper on continuing education indicates that the trend is not confined to women. This suggests once more that the experience of women, who are responding to social change with exceptional sensitivity, should be seen as instructive for all. The return of women to college portends an increasing participation of older people in education, both sexes of them, and at all levels.

Which brings us again to a consideration of the value of flexibility in the outlook of institutions of higher learning, and of their faculties. In "Why Women Go Back to College," Pat Durchholz and Janet O'Connor note, "In some publicly supported colleges, these women make up as much as 10 percent of the student body." A 10 percent increase in possible students would certainly be a boon to many an institution looking at a decline in applications, though we mustn't assume, of course, that such an increase is everywhere available. On the other hand, we shouldn't imagine that the women who have got themselves back to college have whimsically wandered in off the street in response to a selling campaign. On the contrary, older students represent a real potential because so many have had to get themselves on campus under their own steam. Few indeed are the imaginative and innovative institutions which have gone out looking for them, have set up useful guidance programs to help them over the culture shock of entry and acculturation on campus, and have tailored curricula and hours to suit their needs and special demands. In short, what's there is solid.

Once there, what they want is not just to amuse themselves, though certainly some well-to-do women are enriching their lives and stretching their minds by studying "for fun." (So are some men.) But the result of a questionnaire circulated by Durchholz and O'Connor to a random sample of 245 women on two campuses in the Cincinnati area breaks down as follows: 35.4 percent are preparing for employment; 30.3 percent are responding to a need or desire for education or achievement; 25.3 percent are seeking personal growth; 4.5 percent believe further education will promote independence; and 4.5 percent are looking for stimulation. (I should add that my own look at the field indicates that most women returning to college are doing so for a mix of purposes; and often those who go back originally for "stimulation" or "personal growth" end up in demanding degree programs, or preparation for professional careers. They tend to get hooked on ideas, and more and more they enjoy success instead of fearing it.) Records show that the returning women at the University of Cincinnati earn good grades, with both full-time and part-time students achieving B averages. My own findings on these matters agree.

This is good news for students and colleges. What about the bad news? There's plenty. Too many students head for training in traditional areas of "women's work." These areas are often oversupplied, and almost always poorly paid. Teaching from elementary to college level is not a growth area at the moment, but more than half of the sample Durchholz and O'Connor reached were preparing to teach. That indicates a serious lack of career guidance and that, in turn, indicates a fundamental inability on the part of the institution to take returning students seriously. In addition, not many colleges welcome part-time candidates for a professional degree; and rarer still is the campus that offers adequate child care—or any child care, for that matter. This inattention to their needs puts a kind of social limit on the women returning to college. They almost all have supportive husbands; they have to. "Seventy-six and three-tenths percent of our respondents replied that their husbands' attitudes were either favorable or very favorable," say Durchholz and O'Connor. But, as the authors then go on to ask, what happens to the women who run into opposition from their husbands? Answer: they stay home. Not only will they get no support in doing two jobs, studying and running a house, if their husbands refuse to share incomes, or to sign a student loan application, the woman can't make it on her own, for her husband's earnings will make her ineligible for student financial aid.

And what, it may be asked, could or should universities do about *that?* Isn't any dispute between husband and wife over her desire to move outside the traditional family role a purely personal matter? Why should any institution intervene? What has it got to do with education?

There are two answers: one from the women's point of view, and one concerned with the interest of the institution of learning. For women, the *privatization* of their needs and ambitions isolates them from help. "That's your problem," says society or its representative organization, in this case the college. "Cope with it by yourself, each one of you." To a Depression drop-out who remembers the 1930s well, this response is hauntingly familiar. It was what Washington told the unemployed during the Hoover Administration. The Administration was distressed about the problem, but it didn't see what it could do to help. Unemployment was a private matter, between a worker and his employer. Result: the Hoover Administration rapidly found itself removed from office and replaced by a Roosevelt team that was at least willing to try to cope. For the first time, unemployment was seen as a public, governmental problem. Solutions were still hard to come by, but someone was finally asking the right questions. Hoover's failure was not one of morals, but of perception.

It is that kind of failure that is haunting today's institutions of higher learning: lack of perception, lack of imagination. This may seem an odd and even an unjustified criticism today, at a time when superior male universities and colleges have accepted women as students, when their presence and that of applicants from minority groups is growing in professional schools, and when experimental programs and new branches of study are being undertaken. The trouble is that all too often these changes are made perforce, against the grain; and because they are entered upon in a spirit of sullen indifference and even resentment, the great potential benefit of such changes for all segments of academia is not recognized. A chance for real profit is deferred and perhaps lost. Women, minority males, and experimenters have something important to say to their colleagues. They look at the universe of teaching and learning from a new angle. They have special knowledge of The World Out There, beyond the gates of the institution. Consequently they bring more than a quantitative addition of bodies to the talent pool. They bring also a qualitative increase in what is known, what it is significant to communicate to coming generations. By definition, since it has not been publicly recognized before, this knowledge comes out of private experience. But to dismiss it on such grounds is wilfully to choose ignorance.

Fifteen years ago, black experience was still being dismissed in this way. Ghettoes are very private; those who move outside them become "invisible men." But who today would want to minimize the effect and extent of the waves of knowledge that have broken through the ghetto walls and made us look, not just at black history but at urban culture, at the experience of poverty, at all of *white* economic and cultural history in this country, with new eyes? When black knowledge ceased to be private, it set in motion a fundamental reassessment of the whole social mythology of our civilization.

There is no doubt that women's experience will also produce a profound effect. Even those 20-year-old efforts to adapt the college curriculum to women's needs, as then perceived, pointed to *something* in women's lives that demanded attention. The effort to deal with the problem by making education for women more special and private proved to be exactly wrong; but it was evidence that some disturbance was being felt. The compass is swinging round now, but it will go still further before it completes its course. Today, women are allowed to study the full, traditional male curriculum, and to teach it as and where they can. What has not yet taken place is the process through which they will refresh and extend the curriculum, out of the substance of their lives, past, present, and to come.

The "privatization" of women, then, is not a private matter. Rather, it lies at the heart of the difficulty that the Establishment feels about incorporating them into itself. (And not only the Establishment. Kate Millett's report on how the peace strike came to Smith and Vassar makes clear that the revolutionary male is no readier than his middle-class mentors to see his revolutionary sister as a full-fledged comrade.) Articles collected here note how women in professional organizations of scholars have been welcomed as dues payers and passed over as possible officers. The field of women's studies is often regarded with suspicion and distaste, or shrugged off as a ridiculous boondoggle. Catharine Stimpson's report on its birth and growth is thoroughly realistic about the intellectual and financial opposition these programs face, and the hesitancy which still hampers their proponents, who are largely untenured and thus badly equipped to be crusaders. (I note with pleasure, however, that the University of Chicago Press has just asked Professor Stimpson to edit a new journal which will deal with scholarship in the women's field, certainly an influential vote for the solidity of the discipline.)

In general, the position of the Establishment is a grudging acceptance of the presence of women, an acceptance enforced to some extent by government antidiscrimination orders, but certainly not a warm and welcoming hospitality. There are a number of reasons for this aversion and if we are to deal with it successfully, they are worth looking at. The Mandarins don't want us, in the first place, because they are comfortable, and if you are comfortable, why should you desire change? Then, the change they're confronted with is wide-ranging enough to be disturbing. Affirmative action, in itself, means shifting habits of promotion and of procurement of apprentices and protégés—inviting people in whom one doesn't know. In addition, the presence of women on a professional level of equality forces a rethinking of one's opinions on sex roles and functions, and these tend to run fairly deep. As Ruth Hawkins notes, the male tenured professors who must evaluate women candidates for employment or promotion often suffer "an inability to distinguish between these women and their homemaker wives." Pointing this out is not to downgrade the value of the work of homemakers, but to indicate that they necessarily stand in a different relation to their husbands than do their husbands' colleagues: a *private* relation, please note, which once again reinforces the pervasive view of woman as private creature, unfitted for public activity.

This archaic but still wide-spread assumption not only hampers women as individuals, it also works to discredit their ideas: vide the reaction to women's studies. Women today, including many women who do not count themselves as actual members of the women's movement but simply as professionals who expect rational treatment from others in their profession, confront the academic establishment with the need to change more than recruitment programs. They are declaring that the whole conceptual structure of reality, and therefore of what should be taught about reality, is changing.

Now, the Establishment tends to believe that there is in existence a concrete body of knowledge, already pretty well organized, which our society should communicate to its progeny. Changes in it, additions to it, may be necessary from time to time—but how can *women* (for so long private creatures) have anything serious or considerable to add? What's more, they often are drawn to new teaching techniques; and they react with too easy an approval to those odd figures, distressing to all Mandarins, not only maverick academics but laypersons, fanatics, and rebels, totally uncertified by the laying on of professorial hands, who want to shake up the standard body of knowledge as if it were a cocktail. The hierarchy is being told to change both its habits and its definitions, its understanding of how the world is put together; and making these demands are the Untenured, the Uncredentialed, the Unfrocked, whom it can only regard with emotions that it would be too kind to call mixed.

What can academic women do about this situation? I think they had better go on doing what they're already doing, firmly, ardently, unshakeably. While I can sympathize with the reactions of the academic Establishment and realize that these emotions will have to be taken into practical account, it is my considered opinion that the judgment of the Establishment is seriously at fault. Its members are overlooking major changes which have taken place in society, and which affect both the student body and the body of knowledge which it's important—yes, let's use the hated word—which it's *relevant* for the students to learn. These changes, therefore, can be ignored by the research institutions and the teaching profession only at their peril. Let me offer an example. I take it deliberately, for the comfort of the males in Academia, from a male, and from a source which can in no way be associated with women's influence, or with radical thinking: namely, from the August 1974 issue of *Scientific American*. Urie Bronfenbrenner, professor of human development and family studies and of psychology at Cornell University, contributes an article on "The Origins of Alienation." I quote its opening:

> Profound changes are taking place in the lives of America's children and young people. The institution that is at the center of these changes and that itself shows the most rapid and radical transformation is the American family, the major context in which a person grows up. The primary causes and consequences of change, however, lie outside the home. The causes are to be found in such unlikely quarters as business, urban planning and transportation systems; the ultimate effects of change are seen most frequently in American schools and—not as often but more disturbingly—in the courts, clinics and mental and penal institutions. The direction of change is one of disorganization rather than constructive development.

I shall not go on to summarize Dr. Bronfenbrenner's data and conclusions, but simply point out that these profound changes in the basic structure of family life, "the major context in which a person grows up," and which come from *outside* the family, are the very stuff of day-to-day living for women in America, and have been for years. They concern us at every level, from that of practical coping to that of steady philosophic thought, and on to distress and anxiety. We know about them because dealing with them has been assigned to us as our duty and, be it noted, almost always as our *private* duty. Managing details of daily living is held to be a chore with which women can be trusted— and raising children who can live successfully as mature adults in this changing and challenging society of ours has automatically been included in our duties, without conscious determination.

For years now, we have been talking about the difficulty of fulfilling this demanding obligation without assistance from the community, without support from other institutions, individuals, or groups. In reply we have been told that we are selfishly making a fuss over doing something so easy that our grandmothers and greatgrandmothers managed it with little hardship and no formal training. We have certainly been blamed when we failed, but we get no credit for suggesting that failure is possible. Instead, it's been judged as private failure, probably due to selfish reasons. We could do better if we tried.

Against this background it is indeed a welcome change to discover Professor Bronfenbrenner stating flatly that changes affecting the family are major, are public, and desperately need to receive the consideration of the scientifically-minded community. No woman, I am sure, would take any pleasure in saying "I told you so," for we take no pleasure in having become aware of these problems long ago. But we *have* been pointing them out, and that fact should be recorded without recrimination, just as evidence of the sort of knowledge of social phenomena, in the real world, that women do possess and that deserve the attention of all of us.

The crucial point lies just here. These profound social changes, profound enough to have affected the least reachable element of society, the family, are not simply the business of the women who have been trying to deal with them. As Dr. Bronfenbrenner points out, they affect the children of our society and, through them, other institutions. *It is no longer possible to see the problems of women as isolated and personal; beyond this, it is no longer possible to see the problems as pertaining only to women.* They derive from technological change, from scientific and medical advances, from new styles of living and, above all, from the economic restructuring of society, which have together altered the ways men and women live with each other and raise the next generation. The special knowledge of women, summarized in their current demands and aspirations, can be taken as a portent of social needs that affect the whole community. Just as the shocking rise in unemployment during the Depression years signaled a major and irreversible change in American society, so the experience of women over the last generation, culminating in the protests and reactions of the seventies, points to an alteration of earthquake proportions in our institutions.

If the institutions of learning are going to retain their usefulness and endure, they will sooner or later find themselves forced to take account of the advances, vicissitudes, and shifting needs of the rest of us. The institutions are not immune from these needs, which affect all American society, top as well as bottom. Minority members, the unconsidered poor, and women in enormous numbers are not only sufferers from today's social convulsions, we are also pioneers in coping with them. We are in a position to instruct our instructors out of the grind and surge of our everyday lives; and what we have to tell them is vital and unique.

Let us return for a moment to Elaine Hopkins' comparison of the modern university with the medieval monastery. Hopkins means the analogy harshly, for she sees the monastery as a bastion of tradition and orthodoxy, turning its back on the world of reality and confining its membership to a chosen few. That is part of the history of the monasteries, but it is only part, for they did not always symbolize intractable rigidity. True, they were formed originally by men (and women) in retreat from a world of violence and chaos, but as time passed they came to perform functions quite different from those of a safe haven for the frightened. They not only preserved ancient knowledge, they welcomed new information even when it came from a different culture, as with Arab mathematics. They pioneered new agricultural methods and experimented with land use. They served as entrepots of trade for whole districts. They sent advisors to rulers, from local barons to Charlemagne himself. When it seemed necessary, they did not hesitate to inveigh against these rulers. In short, the monasteries were, at various times and in various places, open, listening, and flexible; and above all, in touch with reality.

So we should not, I believe, despair of their present descendants. Women have both history and reality on their side. Our knowledge of the world as it is is really quite formidable, broadly based, aware of detail, and not afraid to make connections between areas which the traditionally minded see as separate. Our experience makes us interdisciplinary. Well, this is a most useful and needed ability in a fragmented society, and particularly in an educational system where the trend for years has been to know more and more about less and less. Research is valuable—if it is used; and to be used, it must be allowed to connect with other research and, even more, with everyday life. In contemplating women's education, therefore, let us not ask merely what the educational institutions can do for us (they can surely do more than they are). Let us ask also what we can do for them. We can do a great deal by supplying not only talent, but wisdom; and the institutions which first realize that (as some already do) will be the ones best fitted to manage our present problems and confront the future boldly.

The Odds Against Women

By Ruth R. Hawkins

Of all the forms of discrimination in American life today, none remains more pervasive or more invidious than that directed against women. In industry, government and academia, women by and large are excluded from positions of power, as defined by salary, prestige and decision-making authority. There is as much sexual segregation in jobs now as sixty years ago, and although one-third of all women now work, most are still restricted to occupations defined as "feminine." In some instances women have been allowed to take over such previously "male" occupations as elevator operators, or have been recruited for such monotonous new jobs as key punch operators. Occupations that segregate heavily have been growing faster than those that do not. Dale Hiestand, in his study of employment opportunities for minorities (*Economic Growth and Employment Opportunities for Minorities*, New York, Columbia University Press, 1964), shows that in occupations in which incomes increase most rapidly, the acceptance of women is very slow. On the other hand, men enter jobs in which income rises rapidly whether or not they have been traditionally female occupations. Men, for example, now comprise the majority of secondary school teachers, and the nursing profession now wants to recruit men because only then will wages and hours improve.

Women now earn 40 percent of the bachelor degrees awarded, but their degrees aren't much help. Men right out of college are recruited for executive training, while women with the same qualifications are offered secretarial jobs. The American woman's share of the employment market has risen in recent years, but her share of professional and technical jobs has actually declined. Women are found predominantly in the less well-paid, uncompetitive jobs; they are more often overqualified in their work, and their median salary is below that of American men, both white and black. Sixty-six percent of employed women with from one to three years of college, 20 percent of employed women with a college degree, and 7 percent of employed women with one or more years beyond the first degree are sales ladies, office clerks, nursemaids, and household cooks.

Despite professions to the contrary, the academic world is not exempt from such inequality. In 1966, two-thirds of the master's degrees and 88 percent of the doctorates were awarded to men. In 1965, of a total university enrollment of 2.3 million students, two-thirds of the places were held by men; at professional schools, 78 percent of the students were men.

These figures reflect academic quotas on women, higher standards of admission for women, denial of loans and fellowships, discouragement of part-time study, and course scheduling and other procedures geared to the service of men. The percentage of women graduate students shows only a slight improvement between 1956 (28 percent) and 1965 (30 percent), despite the unprecedented overall growth in that period. Alice Rossi, using data from a survey of forty thousand men and women of the class of 1961 three years after graduation, found that ambitious women who aspire to careers meet subtle and overt forms of punishment rather than encouragement and support. In her words, if a woman graduate student shows commitment and independence, faculty men call her an "unfeminine bitch," while women graduate students who are quiet and unassertive are described by their male professors as "lacking ambition." Maria Goeppert Mayer, the only woman since Madame Curie to win the Nobel prize in physics, has said: "I sensed the resentment of the role of women in American academic life so I learned to be inconspicuous."

Graduate schools, indeed, are geared to the career development of men, who generally follow a relatively straightforward pattern with little consideration to their lives off the job, whereas the career and life patterns of women are complex and require greater flexibility on the part of academic institutions. Talcott Parsons' and Gerald Platt's *The American Academic Profession: A Pilot Study* (Harvard Laboratory of Social Relations, 1968) appears to indicate that the intrinsic appeal of teaching to faculty members lies in the ways in which it perpetuates the system in which they are enthroned. Their mission is thus to make others into their own image, and students who do not fit the prevailing donnish mold are discouraged from pursuing academic careers.

It is not surprising, then, that women have a low percentage of faculty positions. Of the 494,514 places in 1964, men held 78 percent. (The percentage reaches 90 percent in the most prestigious institutions.) It was not always so. In 1939, women held 30 percent of the faculty jobs—40 percent in 1879. In the early 1960s, however, 37 percent of the teaching and professional staff positions in colleges and universities were part-time, and women were—and are—heavily represented. In this group, of course, they are the expendables; those who are added or dropped in response to changes in enrollment or budgetary support. In addition, Jessie Bernard's study of academic women (*Academic Women*, The Pennsylvania State University Press, 1964) found that the faculty rank of women is inferior to that of men in all kinds of institutions, despite comparable qualifications and productivity. The median salary of women is one thousand dollars less than that of men. One factor, undoubtedly, is that when men fill a vacancy, they tend to seek people like themselves and do not consider untypical members of the guild, including women. The result is that women, although representing over 51 percent of the nation's population, are virtually shut out of the academic work force.

There are predictions, moreover, that in the 1970s the number of college teaching posts will be lower than the number of PhDs available. In this case, the gap between men and women faculty members will widen, since women have gained scarcely 20 percent of the available places during the greatest expansion of higher education in this country. Further, in the 1970s the number of women seeking employment will be unprecedented. Not only will there be a continuation of the pattern of married women joining the work force as their children reach high school, but with the present decline in the birth rate and longer intervals between marriage and child bearing, there will be increasing numbers of young, childless married women seeking jobs.

In the face of these discouraging economic facts of life, the rise of militant feminist organizations such as the National Organization for Women (career women) and the Women's Liberation Front (undergraduate and graduate women students) is inevitable. Indeed, one could only conclude that American women would be suffering from the most debilitating masochism if they did not begin to organize to end this pervasive discrimination. On many campuses young feminists, learning from the techniques of black militants, are pressing for changes in admissions policy, for courses on women such as that initiated at the University of California at Los Angeles, and for hiring and promotion policies which will ensure that women have better representation in higher education. For example, a group in Buffalo has recommended that the State University of New York establish a college with a balanced faculty of men and women, a campus day-care center and a program of study on women.

The parallel between the treatment of blacks and women by our society was drawn by Gunnar Myrdal in an appendix to his classic, *The American Dilemma*. But it was put more dramatically by Eldridge Cleaver, who views the white man as establishing himself as the Omnipotent Administrator. The black man, sent to work in the fields, became the Supermasculine Menial, while the black woman, wearing Aunt Jemima's bandanna, was deposited in the kitchen, a self-reliant amazon. The white woman, ideally the beautiful dumb blonde, was placed on a pedestal, weak-minded and weak-bodied. "That is why when you get down to the rest of it, the white man does not want the black man, the black woman, or the white woman to have a higher education. Their enlightenment would pose a threat to his omnipotence," Cleaver says.

Feminists are concerned with what happens to the relatively few women who do teach in colleges and universities. (Only 9 percent of the full professors are women.) What are the existing criteria for tenure, they ask, and what should they be? Jessie Bernard's study found that academic women preferred to be teachers and were more concerned with students, while men were less responsive to students than to their professional peers. In the Parsons-Platt study, faculty preferred to give more time to graduate than to undergraduate students, and they indicated that they would ideally invest more time in research and scholarship than in teaching at any level. Academic women publish proportionately less than their male colleagues, and feminist organizations question the necessity of contributing to the publication explosion as opposed to the knowledge explosion to win promotion. For a price is paid by faculty members who follow the conventional focus on publications, honorary awards and committee participation; the price is a lopsided life of all work and little play or family and community life.

> "Isn't it time the university [Alice Rossi has said], as the most farseeing of our social institutions, prepared itself for life in the post-industrial world . . . a compassionate world with the time, the room and the flexibility to create a style of living that permits men and women to live deeply and meaningfully at play and at home as well as at work?"

Aside from publication, what objective criteria exist for evaluating a professor for promotion? None, really. It becomes, then, a question of how compatible are the views of the candidate, his life-style and personal relations with those of the tenured members of his department. In this subjective area, women are disadvantaged. There is often an inability on the part of the judges to distinguish between these women and their homemaker wives. And often the refusal to increase the salary of married academic women is not determined by performance, but by personal resentment of the higher style of life enjoyed by households containing two career people.

The goal of the new feminists is an ideological one: equality between the sexes. They are not interested in tinkering with short-run improvements in the status of women. For practical purposes, a certain amount of energy must be devoted to applying pressure on government and other institutions to undertake specific actions or to cease certain practices. But the long-range objective is to change society. The foundations of role differentiation between the sexes are increasingly challenged by medical and psychological research. If the present arrangements are not justified in psychology or physiology, then is it that our economy forces men to work at persistent levels of efficiency and creativity so that the present family system conveniently supports the occupational system?

College enrollment is expected to jump from 5.9 million in 1966 to 9.4 million in 1976, and this does not include efforts to enroll more students from disadvantaged backgrounds. There would then seem to be a need to develop criteria for effective teaching of different kinds of students: the disadvantaged, the job-oriented, the gifted, and the creative. And the question of men and women faculty members, with their special talents and instincts, is involved. But the agendas of faculty meetings rarely include such issues.

Just as blacks have resisted racial integration when it means becoming white to be accepted, the feminists are not seeking assimilation. They are pressing for a reexamination of the socialization process. No assumptions and no institutions are sacrosanct—not family, church, education, or government. Feminism, in its broadest sense, is part of the ground swell for qualitative change in American society.

The Wives of Academe

By Donna Martin

An experienced high-school mathematics teacher moved to a community of three thousand and in ten years of residence there was never able to find another teaching job. A qualified advertising copywriter married and was unable to find employment except when her husband wasn't working. A PhD in history, head of a college history department, married and moved to the town where her husband was employed, effectively ending her academic career. A trained social worker commutes fifty miles a day in order to practice in the field for which she was trained. What do all these women have in common? Each is a faculty wife, married not only to her professor husband but, in effect, to the institution at which he teaches as well.

Faculty wives may well represent the most highly educated and underutilized source of womanpower in the country. As "captive" residents of their academic communities, they have long been ignored or exploited by the institutions at which their husbands are employed. But one fact stands out amid the recent furor over the sex-discrimination complaints filed against more than 360 colleges and universities. It is that faculty wives, because of their qualifications and accessibility, stand to be among the chief beneficiaries of these complaints and the Affirmative Action programs now being developed on campuses across the nation.

While no statistics on the educational level of faculty wives as a group are available, it is safe to assume that the average faculty wife has, at a minimum, a bachelor's degree. According to the Department of Labor, more than 50 percent of women with four years of college and 70 percent of women with five years or more were in the work force nationally in 1968. Yet a quick survey of any college or university community would show nothing like a corresponding percentage of employment among faculty wives.

Because of the relative isolation of many institutions of higher education, the mobility of the academic profession and the outmoded antinepotism rules that still govern many schools, faculty wives all too often find themselves jobless and homebound. For some, no doubt, this is a satisfying alternative; but for the woman who wants a career, the difficulties of finding suitable employment in an academic setting are deeply frustrating.

Of the major state university campuses in each of the fifty states, roughly two thirds are located in communities with a population of less than one hundred thousand. Probably even more than two thirds of private liberal arts colleges are located in small communities; in fact, many of the most prestigious liberal arts colleges in the country are located in towns that would not exist had the college not been founded there. The isolation of much of the American academic community is no accident; as the historian Henry Steele Commager has pointed out, the founding of American colleges and universities tended to follow the English rather than the European model. In Europe, the great universities were usually founded in the great and most populous cities; in England, and subsequently in America, it was thought that the rural atmosphere lent a purity, a lack of worldly distractions, that was beneficial to the academic mind.

All this means that in a large number of college and university communities the institution itself is the only "industry," and thus the only source of employment for a faculty wife. In a small college community there will be less competition for jobs but also fewer jobs available. In large universities the opportunities may be greater, but so will the competition, and there are simply too few jobs to accommodate the number of qualified faculty wives. For example, in 1972 I was an editor and held one of three editorial jobs at a small university press; our files held many applications from other faculty wives who were highly qualified but who would have to settle for jobs for which they were overqualified or for no job at all.

It might be said that the difficulties I point out are difficulties encountered by any career-oriented woman whose husband is employed in a small town. But academe places other obstacles before the aspiring wife.

Let us suppose that she wants to be a college or university teacher. This is not an uncommon goal for faculty wives, because many of them met their husbands in graduate school where both were pursuing academic degrees with an eye toward teaching. Many others have found themselves compatible with their husbands precisely because of a shared interest in intellectual matters.

A 1960 study by the American Association of University Women showed that about one half of all institutions of higher learning in the United States and over two thirds of all large public colleges and universities had some regulations or policies interfering with the employment of more than one member of a family on the faculty or research staff or in the administration. A study conducted in 1970 by the University of Arizona Chapter of the American Association of University Professors and restricted to land-grant universities showed 74 percent of such institutions still had some written policy pertaining to the employment of relatives. Such rules may range from absolutely prohibiting the employment of another family member to—more common today—a refusal simply to allow two members of a family to teach in the same department. But because such rules are almost always invoked against the employment of wives rather than husbands, they have the effect of discriminating against competent women.

In many cases the dissatisfaction engendered by such rules rebounds against the institution itself. The Arizona AAUP study estimated that before the university regents rescinded the university's stringent antinepotism rules, "at least four able, experienced, established men left...because their wives, themselves highly qualified, could not be employed. At least seven others would have left, and may still leave, for the same reason." In addition, says the study, there were at least twenty-seven faculty wives who are "in every other respect qualified, and whose valuable training has been unavailable to the university." The study went on to state that many other possible "good catches" went elsewhere because their spouses were arbitrarily excluded from even applying for a position.

Even where antinepotism rules aren't a factor, it is difficult to mate two academic careers to one institution. Often when a husband finds a desirable teaching position, a corresponding opening in his wife's field simply doesn't exist.

Virtually every woman I have talked to on this subject has her own particular horror story: the PhD or near-PhD faculty wife accompanies her husband to a college or university and, because of the prevailing rules, a lack of openings in her field or simply because of a petty desire on the part of the administration to prevent any faculty family from earning a double income, is unable to get a job. The stories end variously: the PhD abandons her career or finds a job as a file clerk; the near-PhD decides it's pointless to pursue her degree and gives up all ambition of becoming a college teacher herself; the marriage breaks up.

Even if she manages to find a college teaching job, the faculty wife is likely to encounter the general academic discrimination against members of her sex. Her chances of achieving senior rank are poorer than those of her male counterparts: women, who make up 19 percent of college faculties nationally, constitute only 8 percent of all full professors and 15 percent of associate professors. (In 1971 Harvard didn't have a single woman among its 411 tenured graduate-school professors.) Her salary, too, is likely to be inferior. At the University of Kansas, for instance, the average difference in compensation between male and female faculty of the same rank is $2,000. Nationally, according to the Women's Equity Action League, about 50 percent of male college teachers but only 12 percent of female teachers make over $10,000.

But suppose the faculty wife is neither so bold nor so foolhardy as to choose the same profession as her husband's. She will still probably find that her profession is in some way incompatible with his. Until very recently the faculty turnover at institutions of higher education was about 20 percent, with the turnover among junior nontenured faculty running as high as 40 percent. A wife who was "working her way up" in an organization might suddenly find her husband seeking greener pastures. End of job.

With the academic job market tightening up, academic turnover will undoubtedly decline. Even so, outside of academe itself, only public-school teaching is compatible with the calendar. One of the most attractive things about the academic profession is its lengthy Christmas holidays, its summer vacations, its grants and leaves of absence for research, its sabbaticals. The faculty wife who is a doctor, however, finds no corresponding hiatus in the illnesses of her patients. The journalist is not apt to have long breaks between deadlines. The woman in business is not likely to be granted a sabbatical. Very often, when a husband changes jobs or takes a leave of absence, the faculty wife has no alternative but to resign, sometimes on the eve of an important promotion or raise. Such practices are then turned back against them by men who say, "Women are not dependable workers." Yet this situation exists because women try to accommodate themselves to a society in which the husband's livelihood is the predominant consideration.

If a wife accepts this condition as a "given," she must, I think, be vocation- rather than career-oriented. By this I mean that in the realm of work she must think in terms of her skills and interests rather than of her rise within some organizational or professional structure. And further, she must broadly define her skills and be always ready to adapt. Had I, for example, considered myself strictly a scholarly book editor, I would have been out of luck in two of the communities in which my husband has taught.

Instead, I have worked on everything from alumni magazines to organizational newsletters to the Kokomo High School telephone directory.

Some faculty wives, however, are not so flexible. A friend of mine, a near-PhD with college teaching experience, annually sends job applications to some fifteen colleges and junior colleges within a radius of fifty miles of her husband's university and annually finds no openings. When I gently inquired if she had considered teaching in high school, she replied, "I'm interested in the discipline of history, not the discipline of adolescents." Such a statement is apt to rankle high-school teachers who find their jobs rewarding, but upon reflection I realized her response was valid. She is a specialist who has worked many long years to develop her specialty and has as much right to specialize as her faculty husband. The willingness of a faculty wife to compromise is, obviously, an individual matter.

There are other ways, of course, to overcome obstacles against women. A couple may not necessarily accept the "given" that the husband's livelihood is the determining factor. Increasingly, faculty couples tend to emphasize the wife's career as much as the husband's. In some cases good fortune allows a faculty wife and her husband to find compatible and equally satisfying jobs. The trend in recent years toward developing urban branches of state universities and urban community colleges will undoubtedly provide more job opportunities for both husband and wife in the same community. In cases where their job interests aren't compatible, the husband may be the one who is willing to compromise, or accept changes the wife wants. Some couples actually alternate in compromising on behalf of the other's career.

There are other promising hints of change that make the prospects for the faculty wife of the future less bleak than in the past. Antinepotism rules are certainly going to fall. Recently a statement against antinepotism rules by Committee W of the AAUP was adopted as official policy by that organization. This action will add the weight of authority to the opinion already expressed by most of those polled in the Arizona AAUP study that such rules serve no useful purpose. Further, written antinepotism rules can often be legally challenged. In the spring 1972 AAUP *Bulletin*, Heather Sigworth states that "successful legal attacks on antinepotism regulations at state-supported educational institutions should be possible."

Finally, as a result of a recent executive order, many universities are formulating Affirmative Action programs pertaining to the employment of women, under the threat of losing federal contracts where discrimination is found to exist. (See "Race, Sex and Jobs," *Change*, October 1972.) Definitive national guidelines have just emerged. Even so, the Department of Labor, which has delegated authority to investigate college and university cases to the Department of Health, Education and Welfare, has binding regulations to enforce the executive order, and many universities have already had federal contracts held up. Universities anticipating formal demands are trying to increase the percentage of women on their faculties and staffs and to upgrade women's positions and salaries. Faculty wives may count on being prominent among those such institutions actively recruit. Women at schools that have made no progress in this direction can organize and demand that the school institute an Affirmative Action program. If they still meet with reluctance, they can follow the procedures established by the Women's Equity Action League (WEAL) or utilize the provisions of the Equal Opportunity Act of 1972 (amending the Civil Rights Act of 1964) or other legislation enabling them to file a claim against the college or university discriminating against them.

The faculty wife today at least has more options than she had a generation ago. Like the biblical Ruth she may say, "Whither thou goest, I will go," and resign herself to whatever alternatives are open. Or her husband may recall that he also said his vows "for better or worse" and accept the fact that her "better" may well be his "worse." Or perhaps she will find opportunities with newly established urban institutions, or through the demise of antinepotism rules and the active recruitment of women resulting from Affirmative Action programs. Utilizing the talents of faculty wives more fully would benefit not only the wives but academe and society also.

The Rhodes: Still Blocked

By Angela Stent

When Cecil Rhodes, Britain's greatest empire builder and noted misogynist, died, he left behind a testament which embodied his imperial vision. Rhodes's dream was to bring to Oxford University young men from America, the British colonies, and Germany who had "qualities of manhood, truth, courage, devotion to duty, sympathy for and protection of the weak, kindliness, unselfishness, and fellowship." In the years that have passed since Rhodes's death in 1902, the Rhodes scholarships have become the best pedigree that an aspiring male member of the American elite can have, a prestigious key to positions of power and influence within the American establishment. But this access to the corridors of power has become a subject of increasing controversy, and there may be no more Rhodes scholarships if the protagonists of equal opportunity win their legal battle.

In 1973, a bright, athletic Radcliffe senior named Ro-Ann Costin spent many nights in the bowels of Harvard's Widener Library poring over the six testaments which Rhodes left behind. She decided as a result of her research to apply for one of the scholarships, which pay fees at Oxford and provide a living stipend for two years. In many ways she was the perfect candidate—an all-American swimmer, a member of the Radcliffe crew team, and a good student. But Ms. Costin is also a woman. In fact, she was one of three women selected by Harvard to apply for a Rhodes that year in a direct challenge to the will, which states quite clearly that "males only" may apply. The response of the American Rhodes selectors was to ignore the women's applications. The traditionalists have won this round of the fight. But Harvard is determined to pursue the matter and, with pressure from other groups as well, may ultimately persuade the Rhodes trustees to make radical changes in their selection criteria.

The Board of Trustees of the Rhodes Trust, however, cannot change the terms of the will, and thus the whole issue has become extremely complicated. Until 1916, they had complete discretion over the terms of the will, but after the outbreak of World War I, national sentiment in England forced them to discontinue the German Rhodes scholarships. In the face of the international ramifications of this action, the trustees introduced a Private Members Bill into the English House of Commons, which "revoked and annulled" the German scholarships. Since then, Rhodes's will has become subject to the jurisdiction of Parliament. Two more Rhodes Trust Acts were passed, one in 1929 and another in 1946, and now the will can only be changed by an Act of Parliament.

Although Harvard's challenge has been the most concerted, this is not the first time that the Rhodes selection process has been questioned. The pathbreaker was Eileen Lach, a talented student at the University of Minnesota, who applied for a Rhodes in 1972. "My decision was mainly a scholarly one," she explains. "I knew I wanted to study international law with a certain professor at Oxford and this seemed the best way to get over there." Ms. Lach received the full endorsement of the University of Minnesota. The next step for any candidate is an interview with a state committee. Each state committee may nominate two candidates who then compete in eight districts, which each choose four recipients for the scholarships. One month before the interview scheduled by Ms. Lach's state committee, William Barber, secretary of the Rhodes Scholarship Committee in America, wrote to her saying that he had instructed the Minnesota state committee to void her application because "the published rules of eligibility are not satisfied."

Malcolm Moos, then president of the University of Minnesota, later wrote to the Rhodes scholarship committee in Oxford urging them, in the light of current national educational guidelines, to allow women to apply for scholarships. In the meantime, Ms. Lach did have an interview with her state committee, although they made it clear that she was not being considered as a candidate. "We bandied about the issue," she says, "and we discussed social change in general and guinea pigs in particular."

Unlike Ms. Lach, Ms. Costin decided to apply for a Rhodes partly as a matter of principle. She was convinced that Rhodes's will had been misinterpreted. "By 'qualities of manhood,' " she explains, "Rhodes meant the ability to give strong moral leadership, irrespective of sex." She was disappointed by the conservatism of the trustees: "The foundation is supposedly looking for qualities of leadership but they won't recognize the abilities of women."

After Ms. Costin had decided that the Rhodes was the best scholarship for her, she went to her senior tutor and asked whether she could apply. The tutor then took up the matter with Katherine Hutchins, director of fellowships for Harvard, and they decided to discuss the issue with the Rhodes Committee at Harvard. The committee then decided to support

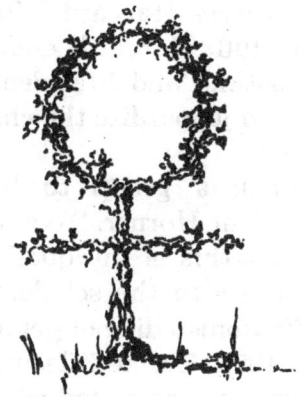

three women candidates, one of whom was an all-American tennis player, thereby opening a Pandora's box of complications and controversy. The committee deliberately took this step "to dramatize the larger issue of academic discrimination against women," as one member put it. "So many women are talented and capable, and we hope that other universities will join us in challenging this restrictiveness."

Unlike the University of Minnesota, however, Harvard did not endorse the women candidates in the normal way. Instead of sending a list of names (usually six or seven Harvard applicants successfully compete for the 32 Rhodes scholarships every year) to the state committee from the candidate's home state, Harvard sent the women's records to all 50 state committees. Harvard President Derek Bok and Radcliffe President Matina Horner sent a letter accompanying the women's dossiers, saying that they wished it was possible to nominate the women formally, that they realized this was an unusual action, and that they urged the state committees to pressure Parliament into changing Rhodes's will to include women Rhodes scholars. President Horner, herself a vocal advocate of women's rights, went to England and contacted the Rhodes trustees about the matter. However, the women applicants were distressed that they did not receive Harvard's full support. "We weren't given full Harvard endorsement," complained Ms. Costin, "and President Bok misled us. He didn't want to jeopardize the chances of the male applicants."

"We can't ask a group to behave illegally," countered President Horner. "We just tried to make them realize that this is the quality of people who should have access to the scholarships."

The Radcliffe women did not get as far as the state committees in 1973. Unlike Eileen Lach, they never heard anything from them, and while the male applicants received acknowledgments of applications and interview schedules, the women were not even given the courtesy of an acknowledgment. "The girls did not really apply," says the secretary of the Massachusetts Committee. "Instead, they submitted a partial statement of their accomplishments." Not surprisingly, the women disagree. And they hope that other women will continue to apply in the future.

The main problem with the Rhodes issue for would-be women applicants is trying to locate both the main centers of opposition to women applicants and the groups responsible for changing the law on both sides of the Atlantic. After the latest Harvard move, William Barber said angrily, "As guest beneficiaries of this scholarship, American colleges have no right to violate the criteria for eligibility." He has vowed to continue to disqualify all women applicants, and most Americans involved with the Rhodes scholarships say they can only fulfill British stipulations and have no business challenging the will.

Don K. Price, dean of Harvard's Kennedy School of Government and the only American Rhodes trustee, also opposes Harvard's attempts to promote women Rhodes scholars, although he dislikes the tactics more than the ultimate goal. He has "the strong impression" that the British trustees support opening the Rhodes scholarships to women, but their hands are tied by the Act of Parliament. "The British government is more concerned with coherent policy than the American government," he claims, and it is therefore unlikely that the Ministry of Education would permit the introduction of a Private Member's Bill just to change the 1946 Rhodes statute. The bill would have to be part of a more general act repealing a number of restrictions in deeds of trust, says Price, "and I don't think anything like that will happen soon. British trusts are not as free as U.S. trusts; and although it's theoretically possible to change Rhodes's will, there are practical problems."

Harvard's general counsel, Daniel Steiner, who has been asked by President Bok to look into the legal aspects of the issue, agrees with Price's interpretation. "There is some sentiment in England for dealing with the problem of sex and education in one fell swoop," he says, "but it's a very difficult problem. Putting aside the morality of the case, it would be possible to continue with male-only scholarships."

Price also questions the political wisdom of challenging the British Parliament: "This is hardly the time for Americans to moralize to the British and issue public statements with a high moral tone. If I were a British trustee, I would take a very dim view of that."

His other main quarrel with Harvard's current stand is that the challenge is inappropriate not only because of domestic American politics but because of the situation of women at Oxford. "There are so few women at Oxford that to propose that women's colleges accept wealthy, privileged Americans and displace English women is not right. The number of women's colleges is so small in proportion to men's colleges and pressure on admissions to college is so great that any spot allotted to a foreigner would take a place away from an English woman." He suspects "they are less keen to have an influx of American women than we might think."

Price's argument has been reiterated by the American Rhodes Committee. It was one of the main reasons given to Eileen Lach for the improbability of the success of women Rhodes scholars. Yet this argument is highly questionable. Oxford has five women's undergraduate colleges, five coeducational graduate colleges, and five of its twenty-four men's undergraduate colleges have recently gone coeducational, with more to follow. The small number of female Rhodes scholars at Oxford would hardly make any difference to the overall situation of women there. Certainly no English women have raised any objections on this score. Yet misapprehensions persist even at fairly high levels. One HEW official concerned with the Rhodes issue described Oxford as "primarily single-sex," which is hardly an accurate description.

Since women first began to challenge the Rhodes selection process, other American institutions have become involved in the controversy. Gwendolyn Gregory, special assistant to the Civil Rights Office in Washington, is looking into various ways of changing the statute. "If there is enough pressure from the United States, the Rhodes trustees could encourage Parliament to pass an act that would allow women to receive Rhodes scholarships," she explains, "but the American Rhodes Committee wants to know what our final position is and we don't have one." Ms. Gregory seems perplexed by the complexity of the issue: "We are meeting resistance from the American Rhodes Committee," she admits, "but they're not sexist. They take an all-or-nothing view, and they feel impotent. They feel that if they can't give it to men only they will have to give it to no one."

The perplexing question Ms. Gregory's office is trying to resolve is whether American colleges that endorse male Rhodes scholarship candidates are violating Title IX of the 1972 Education Act, which bars sex discrimination by educational institutions receiving federal financial assistance.* If HEW decides that selecting male Rhodes applicants constitutes "sex discrimination," then it can threaten all colleges participating in the Rhodes scholarship program with federal fund cutoffs. "The only power we have," says Ms. Gregory, "is to say that colleges can't nominate Rhodes scholars any more. And I have no idea how a bill could be passed in England even if we did that." She has had some informal contact with some British women members of Parliament, but has had no contact with the British Rhodes trustees, and seems uncertain about the outcome of the HEW inquiries.

While HEW decides the question of what constitutes "sex discrimination," Eileen Lach has already entered a legal battle over this issue. On March 4, 1974, the Minnesota Civil Liberties Union filed a suit on behalf of Ms. Lach, a graduate student at Princeton, against the University of Minnesota. The aim of the suit is to make it illegal for any public university to nominate students for scholarships, such as the Rhodes, that discriminate against women. They hope that such a ruling would force the British Rhodes trustees to amend the Act of Parliament to include women, if the alternative is no Rhodes scholars from the U.S. at all. "We are using legal methods to bring about political pressure," says Ms. Lach, "but I think it will take five years for anything to happen."

So far, all efforts to change the Rhodes statute

---

*In summer 1974 HEW published its proposed guidelines, which exempted single-sex scholarships, such as the Rhodes, from regulation under Title IX. At this writing, November 1974, the regulations are being revamped, and their ultimate provisions are still in doubt.

have been unsuccessful. Yet Harvard's Katherine Hutchins is still optimistic: "The response from the trustees has been good.... But the problem is that the trustees can't use money from the endowment to present a bill to Parliament to change the law." A 1974 meeting of Ivy League university presidents delegated to President Bok of Harvard the responsibility of studying the Rhodes issue. His general counsel, Daniel Steiner, began looking into what it would cost to amend the Act of Parliament and how the money could be raised in this country. Ms. Hutchins also encourages former Rhodes scholars to write letters to the Rhodes trustees and to the state committees urging them to change the statute.

For the time being, however, there will be no women Rhodes scholars, though the Harvard fellowships committee urges other colleges to nominate women for the fellowships in order to maximize the pressure. The Rhodes Trust has established a few Rhodes fellowships for women, which are reserved for senior research scholars, but these are separately administered and financed from a special fund and are in no way analogous to the Rhodes scholarships. It will take a major effort on the part of the American selectors to change the law, and they are waiting for guidelines from HEW.

When Rhodes first envisaged his imperial dream, women did not figure prominently in it. But the empire has fallen. And so may some of the old imperialist's prejudices.

The Uncertain Progress of Affirmative Action

Charles J. Sugnet

The faculty club at the University of Minnesota is called the Campus Club, and it occupies the top three floors of the six-floor student union building overlooking Minneapolis and the Mississippi River Valley. Although the anonymity and the geographic dispersal of a large urban faculty have made it largely a lunchtime cafeteria, vestiges of clubbiness remain. Members must not only have assistant professor status, they must be nominated by two current members. Since cash purchases are not allowed, only those who belong may use the facilities.

On the fifth floor there is a large reading room of the gentleman's club type. Off the reading room are billiard and pool tables, and upstairs, where there used to be bachelor apartments for a few male faculty members, there are now small dining rooms that can be reserved for lunchtime meetings.

Many administrators and senior faculty, especially those heavily involved in university governance, come regularly, and a good deal of university business gets done there. Such a place ought to reveal something about the nature of power in a big state university, should tell us whether much has changed since affirmative action became a mandate.

The people in the dining room the day I went in 1974 were mostly white and male, most of them between the ages of 35 and 55. Although the beards, turtlenecks, and rumpled clothes made it impossible to mistake them for a group of businessmen, the colors were surprisingly conservative. Here and there a middle-aged peacock called attention to himself, or a professor's clothing proclaimed him European. But the room was dominated by grays, browns, dark greens. Although Minnesota and the Dakotas have a large Indian population, and although Minneapolis-St. Paul has a sizeable Indian ghetto, there were no native Americans in the dining room—nor can I recall ever seeing one there, though there are a few on the faculty.

Probably a fifth of the diners were women, but many were not full-time faculty members. Two were staff aides to administrators, charging their lunch on the boss's card. An older woman across the room was simply having lunch with her husband, a full professor. The two women arguing at a small table in the corner were newly hired assistant professors, who presumably know that national statistics show their chances of achieving tenure are much lower than those of men in the same position.

A young black couple whom I hoped would prove examples of a changing faculty searched unsuccessfully for the cloakroom and then stuffed their coats into an easy chair in the hall. They'd clearly never been there before and soon were greeted by a Scandinavian woman whose guests they obviously were. Of the 200 or so people who passed that noon, 4 others were black. One was a civil service bureaucrat; the remaining three may have been teachers. In short, if the faculty club at the University of Minnesota is a fair indication, the presence of new faculty people is marginal.

In 1968 the board of regents adopted a statement

endorsing affirmative action employment, and as early as 1969 the administration was considering steps that would give the statement practical force—steps such as nationally advertising all academic positions. But it was not until the academic year 1971-72 that affirmative action became a public issue at Minnesota and the policies that now exist were instituted. HEW had shown it meant business by seriously threatening to withhold funds from the University of Michigan. Minnesota had been notified that an HEW team would visit the campus to conduct what they call a compliance review, and that fall the administrative memos had an urgent tone. Expected daily for about six months, the compliance review team never arrived. But in December of the same year, the Labor Department issued Revised Order No. 4, which spelled out in considerable detail what constituted an acceptable affirmative action program. The university issued a series of administrative memoranda, and one of those established an office for a person to lead its efforts to satisfy federal guidelines.

Lillian Williams now fills that office. Previously a coordinator of the university's compliance efforts for construction contracts, Mrs. Williams reports directly to the president who, she says, has never failed to support her. Until recently, she had a secretary, a part-time student assistant, and a public service careers trainee. A full-time aide has now been added. With this staff, the office prepares plans, goals, and supporting data for HEW, produces a hefty annual report on affirmative action progress, monitors compliance on university hiring—including construction contracts—and of course takes up cases of alleged discrimination that come to its attention.

The office has survived its first years, has served as a focus for complaint, and has had some effect on hiring. But apart from the problems of dealing with issues so complex with so small a staff, Mrs. Williams is obviously in an ambiguous position. Her office exists both to assure HEW that the university is complying with its regulations and to promote affirmative action hiring within the university, and the two purposes are not always compatible. Mrs. Williams, for instance, is reluctant to make public certain figures on hiring, though their publication would most likely increase the campus pressure to hire women and minority people. Such figures might, at the same time, alert HEW to a situation the university prefers to keep quiet.

Further, such efforts as hers are largely ad hoc. If a situation is brought to her attention, she will act; but at a university with 49,000 students and 15,000 nonstudent employees, many problems are bound to go unnoticed. Nor has Mrs. Williams or her staff ever worked as academics. They must perforce accept information from others about the mysterious manner in which academic promotions are made and credentials established for certain professorial jobs. And, of course, Mrs. Williams must depend heavily on vice presidents who have power to use it in behalf of her efforts.

The memos of 1971-72 required each administrative unit to name its own equal employment opportunity (EEO) officer, who was to push to hire more women and minorities. Of 171 persons so designated in 1974, all but about 40 were directors, chairmen, superintendents, or associate deans. Those who made employment policy in the past, it seems, continued to do so. And even the committed are asked to take on those duties on top of ones they already have: they are not paid to devote their primary attention to affirmative action work. Nor do they have regular meetings, a newsletter, or any other form of official contact. The result is a structure that exists largely on paper, having a hit-or-miss effectiveness at best.

The memos asked that all hiring for administrative and professional jobs be halted until each department had analyzed its work force, decided what deficiencies existed because of past discrimination, and set goals and timetables for remedying the deficiencies. These analyses and goals were eventually forwarded to HEW's regional office in Chicago as part of the university's affirmative action plan. After a year and a half, HEW had neither approved the plan nor objected to it; apparently that office is so understaffed that it was not able to complete its analysis. In the meantime, budget cuts and current planning for what administrators call a "steady-state" university made timetables set in late 1971 outdated.

Once a department had set its goals, it was free to hire but was supposed to open its vacancies first to qualified women and minority candidates. If two roughly equal candidates presented themselves, it was hoped the department would incline to the woman or minority person. In practice, the policy of opening vacancies first to qualified women and minority candidates was interpreted quite differently for civil service positions than for academic jobs. The civil service affirmative action program measured success by the actual hiring of women and minority persons. An academic department was thought to have complied if it went through certain search procedures which constituted a good faith effort to recruit them. The contrast is instructive in several ways.

Since civil service jobs at the university consist largely of clerical and secretarial positions, there were plenty of women in the civil service work force, but the higher-paying administrative and professional jobs were heavily occupied by white males. The problem was how to get minority persons and women into such jobs, and the instrument rather hastily designed to do this went by the ungraceful name of "The Female and Minority Program" (F&M). Certain jobs were classified as F&M jobs, open first to females and minority groups. These positions were advertised on bulletin boards, in the Minnesota *Daily*, and in various minority publications. Applications for the jobs would be taken from Caucasian males, but the Department of Civil Service Personnel would not refer such applicants to the hiring department until it was convinced that a good faith effort had been made to recruit and hire a qualified woman or minority person.

The program was of modest size—slightly less than a hundred jobs a year, but all of them professional level positions—and there were various problems with it. It placed a tremendous enforcement burden on the personnel department and made a large number of enemies for it. Some departments were excused from participation on tenuous grounds, and the program worked better for women than it did for minorities.

Nonetheless, it *worked*. In a year and a half 133 F&M jobs were filled, and only 43 of them finally had to be filled by white males. Seventy-six women, including seven minority women, and fourteen minority men were hired under the program. It was relatively successful because the civil service could translate a high-level decision to hire women and minorities more quickly into action than academic departments could. There was less mystification about credentials and qualifications: each civil service job carries a written description of its duties and requirements. And in spite of the low minority population of Minnesota, it is probable that there really was a greater pool of qualified applicants for the civil service positions than for the positions in the academic areas.

Unfortunately, if the program itself was effective, it was also legally questionable. Several complaints of reverse discrimination were made to the state human rights commission and were settled quietly by the university. The program was never put to a legal test, but the disapproval of the human rights commission and the adverse publicity the charges generated were the major causes of its being discontinued in the fall of 1973.

For the professional civil service positions open in the future, a computerized talent bank is now being assembled. The personnel department hopes to have the names and qualifications of so many women and minority persons on file that no department will be able to fall back on the excuse that there were no qualified applicants. The talent bank will not be used, however, until new goals are set, and no one is sure when this will be done. Nor can there be a substitute for putting political pressure on recalcitrant departments to actually hire some of the people whose names are available.

Affirmative action for academic positions took a different character from that of the F&M program, a character that stressed procedures to be followed. First, administrators compiled a universitywide vacancy list for academic jobs and advertised in such publications as *Academe*, the *Chronicle of Higher Education*, and *Black Scholar*. They indicated in a general way that the University of Minnesota had jobs open and would be happy to entertain applications from women and minority persons. Harried aides to the vice president for academic administration then tried to match incoming resumes with the openings on the central list, but this clumsy procedure was soon discontinued. Informed administrators believe that the advertising almost totally failed to produce applicants whose credentials fit the available positions, and that it had been valuable only as a kind of public notice to the academic world—and, of course, to HEW—that the university believed in affirmative action hiring.

Individual departments were also asked to undertake their own advertising and to ensure that positions were held open for a reasonable length of time, so that all potential applicants could hear about them and respond. Search committees were asked to include minority and female members in their deliberations whenever possible, to formulate explicit criteria for the evaluation of candidates, and to keep records of their deliberations.

On April 1, 1972, all these requests were made formal with the introduction of a document called President's Form #17, which asked a number of questions about recruitment procedures, criteria, and applicant pool. After that date, no appointment could be confirmed unless the appointment papers were accompanied by a completed Form #17 signed by the department head and the appropriate equal opportunity officer. The memo introducing the use of the form asserted that "all nominations would be centrally reviewed" and that "no departments could fill positions" unless they had complied.

During the year or so when there was a great sense of urgency about affirmative action, such central review may have been thorough and vigorous. Until recently, an aide in the office of the vice president for academic administration read the forms, but this practice has been discontinued. In many cases central administrative scrutiny is now conducted by secretaries who look to see that the forms are properly filled out before filing them, so that the process can easily degenerate into mere bureaucratic pencil pushing. Higher-level appointments that must be specifically approved by the board of regents receive ample attention. But this category does not include assistant professors and instructors, who are more numerous and more likely to be either female or black.

Without doubt, these procedures have had an effect. Women have recently been appointed to prominent positions. The assistant vice president for academic administration and the assistant dean for admissions in the law school are women. A black man was recently made assistant director for employee relations, and another is assistant vice president for physical planning. But beyond this, it is difficult to find solid information.

The only statistical evidence showing ethnic and sex data specifically for academic employees is in Lillian Williams' annual report of July 1973, which gives gross statistics for all nonstudent academic employees in 1971, 1972, and 1973. These numbers show that between 1971 and 1972, there was a slight *decline* in the number of minority employees and almost no change in the number of female employees, even with a small increase—about 50 jobs—on the academic staff. In spite of everyone's good will and the stated policy of the regents, not much was being achieved until HEW announced it was planning a visit. The statistics for the next year—the year in which the urgent efforts had their effect—are much more encouraging. The overall academic staff increased by 288 persons, of whom 50 were minority and 97 female.

Still, in an academic staff of over 5,000, these are hardly massive adjustments that will eliminate an historical injustice. The fear that goals would turn into quotas or that white males would be eliminated from the job market seems to have been exaggerated. About half Minnesota's staff increase consisted of white males. Women were added almost exactly in proportion to their representation in the national labor force. Between 15 percent and 20 percent of the addition consisted of minority persons. (During the period in question, ethnic studies departments were being established at the university, and these may account for a fair portion of the minority increase.) If you consider that over half of the university's minority staff members are American Orientals, you see that blacks, in this year of maximum effort, were not being added to the faculty in proportion to their representation in the national population. The statistics show progress, but even with great pressure, it is slow progress.

It is also important to note that these figures include *all* nonstudent academic staff members, a category which at the University of Minnesota includes many entirely bureaucratic jobs which carry the rank of instructor. It also includes a large number of teaching faculty who work part time or have temporary one-year contracts and are not entitled to regular faculty status. The 97 women and 50 minority persons added to the staff were by no means all full-time, tenure-track, teaching faculty who will make a long-run change in the university's policies, teaching, and research. Quite to the contrary, they are likely to be in positions peripheral to the permanent faculty, positions where sudden disappearance is more likely.

In assessing the long-range effect that affirmative action has had on the university faculty, it would be helpful to *know* how many of the women and minority members hired as a result of affirmative action were given regular, full-time, tenure-track positions not funded with "soft" temporary money. It would also be helpful to know at what ranks they were hired. But the university has not compiled the information.

The lack of good data about the academic staff is partly the fault of HEW, which requires compliance reporting largely in what are called EEO #1 categories—very broad classes like "professionals," "technicians," "laborers," and "craftsmen." At the university all the academic employees and at least half the total work force fall into the large category "professional," and much of what is interesting about personnel matters at such an institution takes place *inside* that one category. HEW does not require finer discriminations, and except for the EEO #1 categories, which are well defined, it does not have standard reporting requirements.

One institution in the same enforcement region does report on its academic staff by rank, even though Minnesota does not. Some institutions are asked for information not required of others—in a recent study of graduate enrollments, only three universities in the huge Chicago enforcement region were asked to report. There is, further, a wide variation in the procedures and definitions which serve as the determinants of the data. This not only leads to confusion and inequity, but must also distort the national statistics compiled from such reporting.

Regardless of HEW, the University of Minnesota could have compiled information about the effects of the affirmative action program. Form #17 asked most of the necessary questions, and an analysis of those forms would be revealing: it would describe every person who has been hired since affirmative action began by rank and department. By noting the reasons most frequently given when an affirmative action search failed to produce a qualified woman or minority candidate, such an analysis could provide a list of the chief problems the program has yet to overcome. But administrators insist that such an analysis has never been performed.

In lieu of this, a woman's group on campus has scrutinized the board of regents' docket and produced some embarrassing figures. For the period they studied, only 3 of 53 appointments to positions of associate professor or above were women, and all 3 of those were part-time or visiting appointments! University officials rightly insist that these figures are incomplete or misleading, but their assertions are undercut by their failure to come forward with the complete and accurate data that could easily be adduced from the Form #17s they have on file.

The university did not compile base figures showing the distribution of women and minority people by rank, department, and tenure status so that the effects of the program could be measured. Surely any program that took itself seriously would need such figures to remind departments annually of the composition of their work force. Nor has an attempt been made to measure the effects of budget cuts on recently hired women and minorities, or to monitor promotions.

The annual reports of the director of equal opportunity have mentioned the need to do a study of salaries to determine whether there are pay inequities based on race or sex, but the study has not been done. The office of the vice president for academic administration is working on a faculty profile which will include salary information, but because it will not contain ethnic information, its usefulness for affirmative action will be seriously limited.

Many members of the faculty and the administration are dissatisfied with the program's failure to live up to their expectations. They cite smaller budgets and greatly reduced job opportunities, which have made it more difficult for affirmative action hiring to have a significant impact on the composition of the faculty. Administrators also refer to the very real limits of what they can do in a structure as decentralized as the university.

The government would reject such an argument, insisting that the administration can and must be held accountable for the university's behavior in such matters as hiring and salaries. Still, the faculty as a whole did not respond with an overwhelmingly positive effort. Unable to see the distinction between de facto institutional discrimination and personal, individual discrimination, many thought that they were being asked to confess to personal prejudice. They insisted their departments had always hired on the basis of merit alone and had always been open to minorities and women. Perhaps more importantly, many academics perceived affirmative action as standing in opposition to merit and quality. The university's official policy statements to the contrary did little to allay the instinctive fear that the faculty was being asked to lower its standards.

Nevertheless, there is no available evidence that departments have been forced by affirmative action to hire inferior or unqualified people. (Recently my own department hired women and minority members who hold PhDs from Yale, Stanford, and Penn.) If such dilution of quality occurred, it may have happened ironically to those who treated affirmative action most cynically. Starting from the assumption that they were being asked to hire a token regardless of quality, such departments may have got what they deserved.

The most frequently given reason for a department's failure to get more women or minority people is that they are not available in that field. In some cases this is true. National statistics show some fields where there are almost no minority people with PhDs and where the number of women is minuscule.

The percentage of women, for example, in engineering is .44 percent, in agricultural economics 1.03 percent, in physics 2 percent, in business and commerce 2.82 percent.

Since the University of Minnesota is not only a hiring institution but also grants prestigious advanced degrees, it seems logical to ask departments that insist there are no qualified minority or female job candidates to do something about recruiting talented women and minority graduate students. In fact, an affirmative action statement regarding graduate student recruiting has been approved; a modest amount of money has been made available as a matching fund to departments for the support of minority graduate students; and a full-time equal opportunity coordinator has been hired by the graduate school to do recruiting, admissions counseling, financial aid advising, and so on. A recently compiled list comparing advanced degrees awarded to minority persons in 1972-73 with expected degrees for the period 1974-77 shows a considerable improvement.

But serious problems still exist. The amount of money available for financial aid is inadequate; it is only enough to support about 30 students. University figures show the perseverance of the unfortunate pattern where women tend to be a smaller percentage of doctoral candidates in any given field than of master's candidates. In language, literature, and the arts, 56 percent of master's candidates are women but only 36 percent of doctoral candidates are. The figures in social sciences are 39 percent and 19 percent; in education and psychology, 60 percent and 35 percent; in health sciences, 35 percent and 14 percent. Very few women and minority persons are currently entering those fields where they are most underrepresented.

The law school and the medical school are run separately from the graduate school, and their performance will probably have a greater impact on social problems in the United States. Within the last few years both started programs for minority recruitment. The programs are modest: the law school admits 10 to 20 a year; the medical school accepts about 20 such people. Attrition rates so far are low, and both schools seem to be following the progress of their minority students carefully to help keep them in school. Nothing formal is being done to help women, but their percentage of enrollment is rising.

Future prospects for Minnesota's affirmative action program are difficult to assess. There is a pervasive tendency for the last hired to be the first fired, so that a serious budget crisis would wipe out the slender gains of the last few years. The factors that have inhibited the promotion of women and minority faculty members in the past will presumably continue to operate, and low budgets will continue to reduce the impact of affirmative action hiring. But barring severe crisis there is little reason to expect a massive erosion of past gains. It is possible, however, that one or more ethnic studies programs may be abolished in the next few years, and the effect of this would be to reduce drastically the number of faculty members from minority groups. Harold Chase, the academic vice president, said the university would do its best to protect tenure. But faculty members must be affiliated with departments or programs, and he has compiled no information about how many minority people hold credentials likely to be acceptable to conventional departments.

More crucial than financial problems to the survival of affirmative action goals, however, is government pressure, and the intensity and seriousness of HEW enforcement activity have declined very greatly. Morale in the HEW offices for civil rights is so low that people are willing to tell perfect strangers how their enforcement efforts have been frustrated by higher government officials. It seems clear that HEW's civil rights effort is not likely to be given the staff and legal muscle it needs until the national administration changes. And there is no way to predict what the priorities of a new administration will be. The sense of urgency that inspired social change in the sixties has decidedly waned.

Since the great activity of the year and a half following fall 1971, the momentum of the university's affirmative action effort has slowed, in spite of the best efforts of Lillian Williams and others. The university is preoccupied with declining enrollment, budgetary problems, faculty unions, and a high turnover among important university officers. Many administrators seem to be waiting for some new impetus on affirmative action, waiting to see what the next phase will look like now that the time for crash programs is past. If a clear case of discrimination came to the administration's attention, it would doubtless act to settle it rather than make the injured party seek a legal remedy. But such easily recognizable cases seldom arise—which is why systematic affirmative action programs were needed in the first place.

The university is unquestionably the best large equal opportunity employer in Minnesota and has done better than many comparable institutions in the country. Still, this means that the national picture is not very good. Minnesota can be seen as a place where a genuine effort has been made, where there have been real, if tenuous, results, and where affirmative action's future is at best uncertain.

The New Feminism and Women's Studies

By Catharine R. Stimpson

A curriculum, like a globe, pretends to map reality: it codifies the categories to which the phenomena of life have been provisionally assigned. Women's studies, a term that provokes both confusion and contempt, is an ambitious attempt to alter those categories. Writing from the perspectives of an assistant professor of English, who was formally educated before women's studies existed but who now teaches a course called "Images of Women in Literature," I hope to dissipate the confusion and to correct the contempt.

Women's studies is but one of several names for a national movement that has neither formal structure nor official bureaucracy. Its other titles include female studies, feminist studies, gender studies, sex role studies and studies in masculinity and femininity. Observers of limited sympathy also call it consciousness-raising for fem libbers, a trivial fad and man-hating for academic credit. Whatever the label, the growth has been quantitatively impressive.

Before 1969, a few women were teaching a few courses and writing a few scholarly books about women. In 1970 Sheila Tobias, an administrator at Cornell and later an associate provost at Wesleyan, edited an unpretentious, loose-leaf volume, *Female Studies I*. Tobias had been an animating force behind a conference at Cornell in January 1969 which gave women's studies much of its initial energy. *Female Studies I*, admittedly incomplete, printed syllabi from women's studies courses taught in 1969-70, when there were seventeen of them. The next year, Carol Ahlum and Florence Howe, the 1973 president of the Modern Language Association, edited *Female Studies II*. It listed women's studies courses taught in 1970-71, and there were sixty-six. Reliable people estimate that the number of such courses that were taught for credit in colleges and universities in 1972-73 was as high as 1,500. A number of noncredit courses abound—exactly how many no one yet knows. In 1972 a student asked me for a copy of the reading list of my women's course. She wanted it, she said, not for herself, but for her mother, who was going to share it with her study club in Texas.

The courses emerge in places as diverse as community colleges and law schools, Diablo Valley College in California and Princeton University in New Jersey. Contrary to popular myth, they tend to be taught to highly-selected students by highly-selective faculties. One study says that even though universities make up only 12 percent of the total population of American institutions of higher education, they have sponsored 42 percent of the women's courses. Apparently, universities enjoy the presence of a number of adventurous women, some of them from the surrounding community, who are willing to start or to enroll in a women's studies class. Apparently, too, the structure of the modern university has the intricacy and flexibility necessary to give innovators a place in which to begin.

Having begun, women's studies is now following those traditional patterns of academic growth that confer both credentials and academic respectability.

At least ten schools offer a large number of elective courses. So does the Five College Program in Massachusetts: Amherst, the University of Massachusetts, Mt. Holyoke, Hampshire College and Smith. Over twenty schools offer "programs," a loose term usually meaning that an office has been set up and a coordinator hired. At least three schools offer a minor, five a bachelor's degree and four a master's in women's studies. Other signs of interest and proofs of support are plentiful. The following list details only a few of them.

• The Barnard Women's Center, of which I am a part, in the first of a series of annual bibliographies, "Women's Work and Women's Studies," listed 1,334 research projects about women, either in progress or published, in 1971 alone.

• Warner Modular Publications is selling reprints of original articles for use in women's studies classrooms. Sixty titles are now on their list, their prices running from 25 cents to $1.50.

• In the fall of 1972, two serious academic journals —*Feminist Studies* and *Women's Studies: An Interdisciplinary Journal*—began publication. Each in large part was the result of the energy and zeal of one woman: *Feminist Studies* of Ann Calderwood, who had no formal academic affiliation; *Women's Studies* of Wendy Martin, an English professor at Queens College.

• In the winter of 1972 the Ford Foundation allocated $325,000 for research in women's studies as one of several projects about women that it was supporting. In the spring of 1973 Ford awarded fourteen fellowships in women's studies to faculty members and fifteen fellowships to predoctoral candidates; they intended to make research grants the next year, at least to faculty. Ford also has a task force to recommend a policy about women's projects the foundation should underwrite.

- In March 1973 the Rockefeller Foundation granted Sarah Lawrence College $140,000 to help expand its master's program in women's history. The college, which also offers undergraduate courses in women's studies, has committed $380,000 of its own to the program. At the same time, it is creating a modest fellowship program for women leaders and activists. Gerda Lerner, the energetic historian who co-directs women's studies, defines as an exemplary candidate a "woman who has been working for social change for women."

The catalyst for a women's studies course is most apt to be a faculty or staff member. However, no single explanation suffices for women's studies. Members of the San Diego women's liberation movement were responsible for initiating what became a program at San Diego State College in California. At Barnard, I saw two students push and persist until two valuable courses made it out of red tape and into the classroom. At schools in which student enrollment, the academic equivalent of a body count, dictates the amount of budget support, student interest in women's studies has kept a course alive after it was taught once.

Yet personal grit and devotion would have been futile if a set of historical conditions had not been present. I teach "Images of Women in Literature" instead of the eighteenth-century novel, not simply because of my training and temperament, not simply because of departmental politics, but because I live at a particular moment. Many of the events of my time influenced my decision to teach that course:

- The women's movement itself, off campus and on. The more active the women's movement is in a particular region, the more likely the schools in that region are to have a women's studies course—a fact that disturbs some who might not otherwise shrink from admitting that connections do exist between

social forces and the academy.
- The movement toward educational reform, which called for more vibrant classrooms and more vital curricula.
- The black movement and black studies, which worked out a model for challenge to higher education on the part of a class that had been outcast from the prestigious centers of education.
- The liveliness of a national tradition which asserted the value of an allegiance between ideas and events, the humanities and humane deeds. It was Ralph Waldo Emerson, giving a Phi Beta Kappa address, not a young feminist picketing a faculty meeting, who said: "Action is with the scholar subordinate, but it is essential. Without it he is not yet man. Without it thought can never ripen into truth....Inaction is cowardice, but there can be no scholar without the heroic mind."
- The antiwar movement, which bred, perhaps inadvertently, a skepticism about the warrior ethos and its relation to current concepts of masculinity as usual.
- The continuing education programs for women, often ignored, which were trying to connect women and academic life.

Some of the most appealing women's studies programs reflect a fertile, if accidental, match between character and history, private will and public environment. I think, for example, of the only extensive program of its kind in the South: that at the University of South Florida in Tampa. Though it began in the fall of 1972 with only four courses, the number has grown each quarter until there is now a three-quarter sequence on "The Image of Women in Western Civilization" and nine other courses. The program director, Juanita Williams, a psychologist whose courtesy masks, but does not hide, a strong will, wants to work next for a concentration in women's studies within a major. Though Dr. Williams is clearly a taut administrator, the program seems free from a tight ideology. Judith Ochshorn, who teaches in the program, says, "There's not one particular style of teaching or relating to students that has to go along with women's studies. I do think there has to be a serious concern and knowledge about the problems of women, and the history of women, and the psychology of women, and the sociology of women. Part of the openness of the classroom situation comes out of how much the instructor, no matter what the style is, is open to learning."

Clearly the University of South Florida would have been a different place if Ms. X rather than Juanita Williams had sat down and written out a proposal which she then helped to navigate through the appropriate channels. Yet Ms. X would have found the same field in which to work: a happily benign administration; an expanding state system of higher education allowing experimentation; a contagious interest in the status of women; and a pool of talented women, from the North and from the South, employed, underemployed and unemployed. Their diversity proved to be a more useful agent of change than a set of shared assumptions about women and habits of behavior might have been.

The rhetoric of its practitioners, the momentum of history and the haphazard ignorance about women's studies on the part of nonpractitioners help to create a misleading sense of the movement as a monolithic one. Its proponents of course agree roughly about certain things. They believe that most of what scholarly attention the academy has paid to women has been ill-spirited or wrong-headed or both. Pauline Bart, the sociologist, cites as one example the propagation of the species of weird theories about the female orgasm. Such a misalliance of grumpiness, trivializing, error and evasion is parallel to the treatment of women in the larger world—which, however, is less self-righteously committed to a self-image of intellectual objectivity than American colleges and universities.

Consequently there is a massive need for corrective scholarship about women and their lives. Nearly everyone in women's studies believes it will alter the way we think about ourselves. Wendy Martin, for example, thinks of feminist criticism as "a major shift in perception," which readers must learn to take seriously. Gerda Lerner suggests that "we are on the threshold of an intellectual revolution as profound as the Reformation, and...we need women trained in a different way from what we have now to apply new categories and modes of thought."

Its supporters agree further that interdisciplinary work is a tool that lends itself readily to the purposes of corrective scholarship. Six out of the seventeen courses listed in *Female Studies I*—those at Cornell, the University of Kansas at Lawrence, Wesleyan, San Diego State, the University of Pittsburgh and Stanford—were interdisciplinary. Such work potentially has several virtues. It assumes that women, as a subject in themselves and as a focus for the study of human phenomena, transcend the boundary of a single discipline. A history of the American family, for example, will hardly tell the full story of my grandmother's life. Further, interdisciplinary work may provide rich, imaginative concepts with which to describe human behavior and sufficient facts to make those concepts palpable and plausible. It can hammer at the narrow specialization that would turn scholarship into hermetic fragments of inquiry. And it offers a model of teaching, research and learning, in which colleagues are colleagues, not competitors, and in which students are fellow workers rather than somewhat backward, if promising, apprentices.

In practice, the questions offered up for interdisciplinary investigation have been good; reports from interdisciplinary classrooms have been provocative. Yet the actual work produced so far has been only mildly adventurous. Members of various disciplines have tended either to refurbish old practices or to speak together at one time about one subject, such as the woman as worker. And the jargon of the political scientist has been as baffling to the literary critic as the jargon of the literary critic has been to the political scientist. The gap between theory and practice clearly reveals the stubbornness of methodological problems more than it does a particular weakness of women's studies itself.

The supporters of women's studies believe, finally, that the classroom in which women have been taught has been intellectually arid. It has exemplified a dictum of Alfred North Whitehead: "In the history of education, the most striking phenomenon is that schools of learning, which at one epoch are alive with a ferment of genius, in a succeeding generation exhibit merely pedantry and routine...they are overladen with inert ideas. Education with inert ideas is not only useless: it is, above all things, harmful...." Psychologically destructive as well, it has been the scene of a sterile drama: Men competing against each other as if intellectual adventure were a cockfight. Male professors unwilling or unable to provide their students with models of self-reform. Women fearful of the consequences of success if they play such strenuous games. Those women professors who have overcome such inhibitions convincing themselves that tokenism is synonymous with excellence.

That classroom is but one element in a network of institutions that have denied women power, privilege, prestige and sometimes access itself. It would be, at best, grotesque to work to get a women's studies program without working to change the psychological, educational, social and political context in which such a program were to exist. It would be absurd for a student to talk about Mary Ellmann's notions of phallic criticism in the morning and then, in the afternoon, to have a historian tell her that the nineteenth-century feminists were crazed spinsters who ought to have been pouring tea or to have a man in the school health service lecture her about the wickedness of abortions. Consequently, women's studies and affirmative action are inseparable goals. Many people in women's studies would agree with Ann Scott, a vice president of the National Organization for Women, when she writes: "I believe that a university must equip women to survive in our world of the overpowering institutions which have historically excluded them (including the university itself). It can do this through adopting a variety of intervention techniques designed for enabling women to intervene for themselves, through using its own resources to intervene for them, and through using its own structure as an arena for training in intervention."

This set of shared beliefs clearly embraces a mixture of hopes. Some are intellectual: women's studies will help us to think better and to know more accurately. Some are psychological: women's studies will help us to behave more humanely—women more freely, men less pompously. Some are political: women's studies will alter power relationships within institutions and between the sexes. A class itself may not engage in political activity—my literature class reads books—but students and faculty often share a sense of political engagement. Such an amalgam of intellectual, psychological and political ends helps to make women's studies less a monolithic movement than a multiplicity of groups.

The people in women's studies differ in temperament, values and in their approach to and ambition for women's studies. Some were pioneers, who took women as a serious academic subject before the new feminism made them a serious public issue; they may still take women as a serious academic subject, but they may not actively participate in the new feminism. Some are ideologues, who were feminists first and who now try to balance their politics and their profession. Some are radicals, who place both their feminism and their notion of women's studies within a large context of demands for revolutionary educational, political and social change. There are the latecomers, who recently discovered that women were an interesting academic subject and whose feminism is often enhanced when their new interest provokes resistance. Finally, there are bandwagoners of both sexes, whose attraction to women's studies is faddish and exploitative, and for whom women's studies may mean little more than writing a paper about the Wife of Bath instead of King Lear. I am an ideologue, who wondered how the insights that drove me on to a picket line might be applied to literature, and who wavers toward radicalism. Character, as well as a stubborn belief in the possibility of institutional change, softens my radicalism.

And I have found teaching women's studies courses exhilarating. For example, my first classes on Virginia Woolf's novel *To the Lighthouse* provoked paradigmatic quarrels among the students. At once moral and literary, the discussion whirled around the character of Mrs. Ramsey. The radicals loathed Mrs. Ramsey, to them a sheltered creature of the *bourgeoisie* who submitted to an oppressive husband's intolerable demands. The feminists were ambivalent. Ms. Ramsey, though she did take on a traditional role, had agreeable virtues: the desire to draw the alienated out of their psychological exile; the desire to unify the fragments of experience. The curious said the novel was a novel, not a tract, and that was that. As the quarrel, which I have oversimplified, went on, I felt the class exert a silent pressure upon me to exercise professorial authority and get it over with. Trying to dispel the notion that a teacher was *ipso facto* a greater authority than a class, I wanted the class to go on until its members had themselves articulated the terms of their disagreement. Finally, we had to compromise.

The men who have taken my course have been at once cheerful, smart, pleasant, modest and curious. Some of them have had encouraging girl friends. My sample is, however, highly selective. Talking about women's issues in general outside of the women's studies classroom but inside of the university community, I have found some male students marvelously receptive, but others either hostile, indifferent or nervous about women in authority. A favorite technique is to lecture uppity women and especially me, as their "representative," about feminism's flaws and failings. And to have a sophomore, who admits that he has never read Marx and Engels about women, announce that "a women's movement" has nothing to do with "the dialectic" strains both patience and credulity.

The questions that provoke internal quarrels, most intense between ideologues and radicals, haunt women's studies program after program. Some questions concern structure. Should a program be a separate department? If so, it may have more autonomy and self-control. On the other hand, a separate department may turn women's studies into a ghetto: older, more established departments may feel free blithely to ignore the scholarly discoveries and teaching methods of the women's studies group.

Other questions are conceptual. Is there such a thing as a woman's *gestalt*, and if so, should a program institutionalize that way of thinking, feeling, perceiving and responding? Still other questions are moral. What kind of person do I picture as the ideal product of a women's studies program? Would I, for example, celebrate if one of my students wanted to become the first woman president of a munitions factory? She would be exercising the freedom of choice that is a principle of the women's movement, but she would be choosing to make guns, which I find antithetical to other deep principles of the women's movement. Am I being either prissy or totalitarian even to ask what kind of a person a women's studies program ideally might produce?

The most perplexing questions are simultaneously structural, conceptual, political and moral. What, for example, is the relationship between a women's studies program and women in the larger community? What might that community be? Any woman in the surrounding neighborhood, or simply women of congenial intellectual concerns? If a women's liberation group in town helps to set up a women's studies program at a local university, should it have a say in that program? Should it have a veto over faculty hiring? Such a problem, for example, created tension between the Tampa Women's Center and the women's studies program at the University of South Florida. The women at the university, if for practical reasons alone, could not grant the women in the community the authority they sought.

What is the tie between a women's studies program and the women's movement? Does the former think of the latter simply as a fascinating phenomenon that history has obligingly cast up, or does someone in women's studies remain, as Marilyn Salzman-Webb says, "more closely tuned to an ongoing feminist movement than to the university proper"? Should a program take foundation money? Such money is useful, even necessary, but such money is also historically tainted. Even the laundering of philanthropy cannot wash out the ways in which great American fortunes were amassed.

The darkening quarrel about theory and practice is a psychological stain: an atavistic distrust that women often appear to feel toward other women who are either successful or have authority. That distrust may express itself in private gossip, public accusations or both. The code words in which the feeling is expressed—star, elitist, establishment sell-out, ripping off the movement—are easily deciphered. Clever administrators who wish to deflect pressure for women's studies as an academic program and for women's equity as an institutional policy—and who wish to do so without openly offending either women or HEW—increasingly manipulate such psychological guerilla wars for their own gain.

Clearly, some tensions are beyond immediate healing, some disagreements beyond reconciliation. Either a community woman has the power to vote on a university faculty member, or she does not. Either a program takes foundation money, or it does not. Either a senior male professor speaks to a 20-year-old traditionalist about chauvinism, or he does not. Yet some disagreements are more inflamed than necessary. It is clearly folly to say that working on a paper about Aphra Behn, that professional woman writer of the seventeenth century, renders me constitutionally incapable of demonstrating for day care during the same day. What may emerge from the women's studies movement is a temporary consensus that each program must work out its destiny; that no single program may claim an exclusive right to sanctity and perfection; that women's studies should be seen as a multiplicity of intersecting activities, not as a limited number of rigid models.

The internal turmoils also shrink in significance

when they are compared to the larger quarrel between women's studies as a whole and its external opposition, which is far more ferocious than a casual observer might suspect. The habit of challenging women's studies either through scoffing ridicule or quiet gossip disguises its virulence. Doubts tend to surface rhetorically as a mixture of pejorative comment and question, and the verbal clusters, if dismembered, reveal some distressing attitudes. One such cluster, "Women's studies is female chauvinism. Aren't they going to study men?," arises from the false assumption that the practitioners of women's studies will simply invert the habits of the past, that women will now exclude the sex that once excluded them. Another cluster, "Women's studies is absurd. What's next? A Department of Male Studies?," reflects a refusal to take women seriously enough to make them a focus for the study of the world in general. A third cluster, "Women's studies is empty. Do they do anything besides scratch each other's consciousness?," ignores the solid accomplishments of women's studies and dismisses the respectable possibility that a liberal arts education might expand consciousness, personal and public.

Some of the sources of resistance are too powerful to be ignored, others too sympathetic on other grounds to be disdained. Institutional conservatives of both sexes dislike any disruption of current curriculum and intellectual practices. Women themselves often distrust any challenge to the notions of sexuality and sex roles that society has offered and they have accepted. Many, but not all, blacks resist women's studies, which seems to them the latest plaything of pampered, middle-class, white women, and a competitor for funds and administrative attention to black studies. The competition among black men, black women and white women for campus jobs affirmative action programs have opened up tends to stir the sour soup of suspicion. Young male faculty members, neurotically convinced that losing to a woman is more emasculating than losing to a man, are legitimately anxious about the academic job market and often too shrewd or too insecure to begin a career with a reputation as a boat-rocker. They may fear women's studies as the opening wedge of a social force that will threaten their personal security, intellectual values and ingrained ambitions.

Behind the resistance, of course, is a deep cultural bias against brainy women. The bias, which implies that women and studies are mutually contradictory, asserts that men are rational, women irrational; men use their heads, women their hearts; men inhabit and manage our great institutions, women the home. The belief is so obviously silly that people often refuse to admit it has influenced them. Certainly, intelligent people of both sexes have long protested against it. In 1792, for example, Mary Wollstonecraft, in the *Vindication of the Rights of Women*, was attacking Rousseau, who declared in *Emile* that women were more or less incapable of reason. The necessity of protest remains.

Given the magnitude and complexity of the resistance, it is hardly surprising that women's studies is still vulnerable. The fact that a majority of the people teaching women's studies are non-tenured adds to the precariousness and instability of the movement. I know of no national count of the number of courses that have been dropped because a teacher's contract has been terminated. Such a statistical blank reveals a need for massive, systematic research into the cause, structure and effect of women's studies as well as for a national office that might help people in trouble on the local level. Anecdotes and case studies do, however, abound.

In the spring of 1972 I heard from a faculty woman at a large, Midwestern university. In two semesters there the women's studies courses dropped from six to zero. The woman had several explanations. Her nontenured slot made her a strategic weakness. There was implicit hostility toward women on the part of the male members of the committee that administered the unit that sponsored the women's studies courses. Other women on the faculty, fearful and indifferent, refused to risk too close an association with something having to do with "women." There was a pervasive distrust of any new program, and students were easily discouraged.

The meeting between women's studies and its resistance is still too young, too much in process, to make its outcome a safe subject for prophecy. Budget cuts may either help or hinder women's studies. In those institutions in which high enrollment dictates a budget, a popular women's studies program will get support. In those institutions in which established departments have the first claim on scarce resources, women's studies may be starved out. At the moment, the proponents of women's studies seem to have the personal energy of many women and some men, the need to meet academic and social needs and a sense of justice on their side. I like to compare women's studies to one version of ancient myth. I think of Athena, who emerged from the head of Zeus, her father, even though he had swallowed her mother in order to stop an uprising of her offspring against him. Despite the fears of Zeus, Athena became a goddess of wisdom and skills, not of rebellious anarchy. At its best, women's studies promises the entrance of Athena into a democratic pantheon, not that destruction of academic standards its opponents so darkly and loosely predict.

The Women's Revolt in the MLA

By Virginia Barber

Ever since the famous 1968 attack by its academic avant-garde, the Modern Language Association has been schizophrenic. Voices demanding sweeping, radical change and voices insisting on the authority of the past have spoken from the same body. The strongest demands for reform have come from women. At the December 1971 MLA convention, held in Chicago, the radical New University Conference was still very much alive, but women's groups were more vocal and apparently more successfully heard. There, change came to MLA, but it is too soon to know if that change will be profound and lasting or just superficial.

In 1969, responding to the women's movement, MLA created the Commission on the Status of Women in the Profession, headed by Florence Howe of Goucher (and now at the State University of New York at Old Westbury). The action had been long in coming. Although women make up one third of MLA membership, they have rarely exercised administrative or executive power. But for many even this step was not enough. With the possibility of a new MLA constitution before them, and with the history of MLA's indifference to women behind them, many women wanted a group aimed at constructive action and feared that the commission would prove merely a study group. The Women's Caucus for the Modern Languages (WCML) was formed with an initial membership of 10, and quickly grew to more than 500 by 1971.

MLA never officially sanctioned WCML. In fact, the women were not allowed to use MLA's name in their title, Yet, WCML has worked well with the official Commission on Women, which itself proved far more than a body generating reports destined for the filing cabinet. The first task of the commission and of WCML was to elect a woman to executive office in the association, one who would actively oppose discrimination not only in MLA but in the profession as a whole. In 1970 Florence Howe was elected second vice president and advanced through the stately constitutional progression that made her MLA president in 1973. Although MLA had had two women presidents since its founding in 1886—Louise Pound in 1955 and Marjorie Nicolson in 1963—it had never had a feminist president.

The second task for the women's groups was to prepare for an elected Delegate Assembly proposed in the new constitution. By some logic not clear to the members at large, MLA leadership chose to pair the names of candidates and asked members to vote for one of a pair in each case. Naturally this process struck some members as a device to pit like-minded candidates against each other (and in at least one case, a member declined nomination because he was paired with a political radical whom he personally admired and whose thinking matched his own). However, nominations by petition were allowed, and delegates to represent "special interest groups"— including "Women in the Profession"—were also put on the ballot. The results of this voting system were gratifying. The first Delegate Assembly, which convened December 1971 in Chicago, was approximately one third female, a proportional representation of the membership, and it remains so today.

The women made other gains with a minimum of difficulty. At one point during the 1971 Delegate Assembly meeting, a man rose to protest that five women and only one man had been proposed for the Elections Committee, which nominates delegates for the special interest groups and supervises elections. He was quickly silenced when a delegate pointed out that the reverse situation had existed for 86 years and no one had objected. Three women and the lone man were then elected as new members to the Elections Committee, which even so was dominated by men, four to three.

To appreciate how sharp a break with precedent these actions represented, one has only to glance at the study of the official MLA Discussion Groups, submitted by the Commission on Women to the 1971 convention. By 1974 there were 68 of these discussion groups dedicated to the study of specialized fields in languages and literature. They are run by executive committees which set the topics to be studied in their sections and select the papers to be read, usually guaranteeing the author publication in a prestigious journal. As the core of MLA, the groups have long been the proving grounds for many distinguished scholarly careers. Yet in spite of the significance of these groups, their executive committees are organized with confusing inconsistency—membership ranges from two to eleven, and term of office from one to five years. The one consistent characteristic, demonstrated by the commission's study in 1971, is the underrepresentation of women. From 1962-1972, for example, the committees concerned with American literature were all male, except for one woman elected in the early sixties. Other committees were not much more egalitarian during the 10-year period 1960-1970: Comparative Literature—113 men, 10 women; English—237 men, 12 women; French—103 men, 6 women; General Topics—153 men, 15 women; Spanish—149 men, 10 women. (Although Spanish was more open than most in allowing women to read papers: 40 of the 192 papers—17 percent—were given by women. By contrast, no women read papers in the Shakespeare section.)

Even for men, merit is not always the overriding criterion for election to these committees. Current members tend to nominate their friends or former students to succeed them, and, predictably, the new members are associated with the same schools—Yale, Harvard, and Columbia—which have long dominated in spite of efforts to move establishment boundaries westward. The committees often have interlocking directorates, too (one man served on three committees simultaneously), and many instances of repeat terms, in some cases reaching toward a decade. As a result of the new constitution, the committees have taken on political as well as scholarly significance, for they each elect a member to the Delegate Assembly, 30 percent of the total. Yet the executive committees remain the real closed societies of MLA.

The surest way to open them up would be to attend their business meetings at the convention and nominate new members from the floor. Yet the women may have damaged their chances in 1971 by allowing their own meetings to conflict with committee sessions. Intent on educating themselves and watching their numbers grow, the women drew off into a separate group and neglected some of the political tactics which might have helped them play their legitimate role in the profession.

Even so, many individual women and other members denied entree into the official power structure came upon a remarkable back door—the annual convention seminars. In 1969 there were 75 of these seminars; in 1974, there were 205. To schedule a seminar, a member announces a topic and finds seven other members who will sign a statement of interest, which is not a vow of attendance. Thus, someone from the most obscure college in the country, perhaps completely unkown to all but seven other MLA members, could then find his/her name on the official program of the meeting as a seminar leader.

MLA found this structure cumbersome, and both discussion groups and seminars were to be abolished at the 1974 meeting. New Divisions would be established; all MLA members would choose a division; and officers were to be elected democratically. Surely the invasion of elite strongholds by the special interest groups and the enthusiasm for the seminars helped motivate MLA to design a new, potentially more representative structure. For women, some gains toward equal representation were assured in 1971 and impressive enough for Carol Ohmann, then chairperson of the Commission on Women, to express "guarded optimism."

Her caution was justified, for many of the women's activities in 1971 centered on unofficial or semiofficial groups. There remained a real question whether the ponderous MLA actually moved toward the women or merely engineered a brilliant illusion. The last may be all that is necessary for an efficient organization like MLA, which is, after all, no stranger to illusion. Witness what happened to the political radicals. Their leader, Louis Kampf of MIT, served as president of MLA in 1971 and delivered his farewell address in Chicago. He labelled MLA a "monster" whose members constituted "an intellectual proletariat." The institutions they serve are products of an "industrial capitalism" and have isolated students and professors in "an autonomous, esthetic realm." Cut off, the institutions will not survive, for "the profession, as the spectacle of our unemployed students and colleagues vividly shows, has begun to outlive its usefulness to the industrial state." The institutions must change, he said, urging members to revolt and "seize control of them," forcing them to participate in the "wider movement for radical social change." At the end of this ringing call to arms, members applauded politely and shuffled out of the ballroom for a nightcap.

The nonreaction may represent the general indifference to issues in the seventies. But there are other factors here. MLA presidents have only a year to effect change and their most immediate contact with the membership at large comes at the annual meeting, marking the *end* of their year of service. Meanwhile, the powerful executive secretary, the treasurer, even the executive council, much like a civil service, stay on and on. If these officers had blundered—say, lost control in 1968 or 1969, or failed to give the radicals at least a hearing—they perhaps would have been turned out. But they did not blunder, and in the case of President Kampf it may be that *plus ça change*...was again in force.

With the women, it could be different. In 1972 they held five of the top fifteen executive positions and were well established in the Delegate Assembly. However, as Florence Howe noted, "The number of women tells you less than you would like to know—you really want to know what's inside their heads." A prescient comment, for in 1974 the Executive Council of MLA had a majority of women, but not of feminists, and the distinction was noticeable.

Difficult as it is to change an institution, Professor Howe's year as president did help to do so. The changes are partly revealed through statistics (the number of women in high places), partly through the number of helpful studies MLA has sponsored or encouraged (*Who's Who and Where in Women's Studies*; an updated *Academic Women, Sex Discrimination and the Law*; *Academic Women and Academic Unions*; *Directory of Women Scholars*; studies of affirmative action plans, of tenure, salary, rank, and how these are attained, etc.), and partly through a new air of confidence. As one officer put it in 1974: "MLA has become one of the most achieving of organizations with respect to women. We've lost our sense of isolation. We're more secure, less frightened about our existence." This is true in spite of the terrible state of joblessness which threatens the life of literature and language departments, as well as the livelihood of individuals. Beyond question, the women's movement has prevented an automatic tapping of women as the "first to be laid off" during this age of cut-backs.

No doubt there are those of both sexes who question the reality of discrimination against women in academia. They should read the report prepared by the Commission on Women and published in *PMLA*, May 1971. The report, based on a scientific sampling of MLA member departments, sets out the relevant facts in statistical charts and concise commentary. In their conclusions, Florence Howe, Laura Morlock, and Richard Berk state, "Women in our profession find themselves, for the most part, in less prestigious, less privileged institutions, teaching mainly freshmen and sophomores, and earning less money than their male counterparts." To quote from only one set of statistics, women account for 31 percent of those receiving PhDs in the last five years, 33 percent of the faculty with full-time appointments but only 18 percent of full-time full professors and 8 percent of faculty teaching only graduate students in departments with PhD programs.

The commission, WCML, and various women's groups are concerned primarily with these problems affecting the profession as a whole, even more than with the internal structure of MLA. With the help of the Department of Health, Education and Welfare and women's groups, colleges and universities are beginning to adopt affirmative action plans to end discrimination against women and minority groups in faculty, staff, or custodial positions. In 1971 MLA proposed such a plan for its own employees. The changes do not come readily (though once achieved, they are often substantial. For instance, the University of Wisconsin has now equalized salaries regardless of sex and has promised to open up promotions and tenure to more women). And while the general atmosphere is less threatening, a single powerful male can still sweep virtually all the women out of his departent as occurred several years ago at the University of Pennsylvania, and women are still fired or find their contracts are not renewed if they support their sisters' cause or "political activism" too loudly. For this reason, among many others, Verna Wittrock, president of WCML in 1971, proposed that the Delegate Assembly appoint an Emergency Committee on Academic Freedom. Because individual cases of discrimination are so common yet so difficult to prove, the major emphasis has shifted to class actions. A number of highly significant cases involving such class actions are now in the courts.

But by no means all the women's news from the 1971 convention concerned structural and legal issues. Since 1969, MLA had offered day care facilities at the convention. Thus, the look of the convention had changed to include a scattering of toddlers, strollers, and infant seats—as well as longer hair and more relaxed dress.

Also, many of the papers read at the convention were on subjects of particular interest to women. In almost every field one or more of the discussion groups selected feminist or feminist-related topics. A heady moment occurred when a WCML meeting learned that in an upcoming session on "Child-Rearing Practices and American Literature," four of the five speakers would be men. There were loud protests and vows to break up the session. Nothing of the sort occurred. Not even an ironic cough from a sparse audience disturbed the all-male panel (the lone woman scheduled to appear was marooned on an island off Maine).

Elsewhere the Experimental Phonetics group heard two papers on "the relationship between sex role and speech." Other papers dealt with "Mrs. Gamp as the Great Mother: A Dickensian Use of the Archetype"; "Women in Spain: Medieval Law Versus Epic Literature"; and women in eighteenth-century French literature. In addition there were seminars on Virginia Woolf, Joyce Carol Oates, and Doris Lessing. (WCML members protested that the Virginia Woolf seminar was to be led by a man, until J.J. Wilson, the leader, rose from the audience and identified herself.)

The topics of the large forums reflected a seeming concern with the kind of issues once shunned by MLA as "fashionable" or "modern" and therefore possibly "ephemeral." This time MLA appeared willing to risk those charges by scheduling forums on Black Studies, Film and Literature, Economics of the Profession and the Job Market, and The Woman Writer in the Twentieth Century.

In addition to forums, seminars, workshops, and individual papers of particular interest to women, there were job raps and legal raps, a showing of the film *Wanda*, several cash-bar receptions sponsored by the Commission on Women, and tables displaying a wide variety of feminist literature. Substantial, nationwide elimination of sexual bias in the profession is still a goal for the future, but the 1971 convention celebrated real gains.

With their new measure of security, women are understanding the relationship between their concerns and other difficult educational issues. Florence Howe is among those who have long seen these interrelationships. In 1971 she said, "The women's movement grew out of the original effort of some radicals to stir things up in MLA, and it has accompanied efforts to make the association more responsible to its membership, 50 percent of whom are now the Vietnam generation. MLA is now full of recent graduates who need jobs and can't find them. This generation has a keen awareness that it is impossible to separate literature from life."

These themes were central to Professor Howe's 1973 presidential address, "Literacy and Literature." Defining literacy as "the power to name the world through the word," she denied that any teacher could—or should—separate the teaching of literacy from the study of literature. As teachers we must accept the reality of bias and our natural subjectivity. These facts are among the lessons learned by the Vietnam generation. We are not "one world," but there is a value in diversity, which our literature embraces. The curriculum must reflect this too. We must no longer assign only books with white male protagonists. We must include those with blacks, women, and others formerly invisible in standard reading lists. Of course, we *do* influence our students and the teaching of literacy and literature matters unequivocally, as both an act of survival and of joy. It is in the context of these broader issues—survival, joy, change—that the women of MLA are becoming equal partners in our beleagured profession.

Women and History

By Bari Watkins

In 1969 it would have been hard to find a senior history major at any American College who had heard of Charlotte Perkins Gilman, a turn-of-the-century feminist. But now it is just as difficult to find one who has not. Ironically, that same senior, if a woman, can look forward to entering a profession almost—but not quite—as closed to her as it was when she entered college. Her experience demonstrates that the women's movement has radically affected the teaching and writing of history, but that women historians have far to go before they achieve employment and salary equality with the men in their profession.

Despite HEW reports, affirmative action, and even the dark forebodings of white male historians, recent reports seem to indicate that women have not benefited as greatly as they had hoped from changed employment practices. On the other hand, and in the face of a certain amount of skepticism on the part of established (and establishment) men, women's historical studies have steered the profession away from traditional fields of politics and foreign policy onto less well-traveled roads.

A glance at the stock of any college book store or

the tables of contents of the leading historical journals reveals the burgeoning interest in the history of women. Book stores have established new sections devoted to women's studies, and most books displayed are centered on women's history. An informal check in an Ivy League establishment reveals a ratio of women's history and sociology over polemics of about four to one. Prestigious journals like the *American Historical Review* or *American Quarterly* and publications in newer fields like the *Journal of Popular Culture* and the *International Review of Social History* devote an increasing amount of space to articles about women's history. In addition, however, there are women who work in other research fields, and from their efforts have come changes in the profession and in historical thinking not solely related to the study of women but to the historical enterprise in general.

The American Historical Association (AHA), a bastion of scholarship and legitimacy since 1884, first felt the effects of the women's movement at its 1969 annual convention. A group of about 20 women formed the Coordinating Committee on Women in the Historical Profession (CCWHP), designed to support the separate but related issues of women in the profession and the field of women's history. Despite its deliberately innocuous name, the CCWHP organized as a caucus for women who were already radical by AHA standards—the day of tweedy and ladylike women historians was officially over.

Coming after the black revolt of the 1960s and the ongoing turmoil over the Vietnam war, the women's movement appeared as yet another shock to the hegemony of traditional historians and traditional history. The CCWHP pushed for immediate reforms ranging from day care facilities at the convention to changes in hiring practices, but acted most importantly as yet another reminder that historians are not remote from politics and that social concerns could be brought to the usually genteel atmosphere of a gathering of historians.

Since 1969, the CCWHP has remained formally independent of the AHA and has developed into a loose network of regional organizations of women historians. It has forced important bread-and-butter reforms on the AHA, which reluctantly established an Ad Hoc Committee on the Status of Women that was later institutionalized as a standing committee. The AHA developed a computerized roster of women historians to serve universities searching for "qualified" women for faculty and administrative posts. It also issued a report prepared under the chairmanship of Willie Lee Rose, professor of history at Johns Hopkins University, documenting the extent of discrimination against women faculty members in a range of different types of colleges.

It was little comfort to women to learn from the Rose Report, for example, that the prestigious Yale department has had only one woman full professor in its entire history. A later study by the West Coast Association of Women Historians demonstrated that in 109 history departments in the Western states, fewer women were employed at the end of the decade of the 1960s than at its start.

The efforts of women's groups of all kinds, of course, have begun to alter that dismal picture, but many women fear that recent job openings at the junior faculty level are actually revolving door affairs, where two- or three-year contracts are offered to satisfy popular demand and the HEW, but from which few women will ever be promoted to tenured slots.

The CCWHP continues as a watchdog on the AHA and the Organization of American Historians, fielding candidates for AHA offices and pressuring for further reforms in the profession including increased hiring of women a reconsideration of undergraduate teaching, and that *bête noire* of gentility, unionization of faculty members. Reformism aside, it seems possible that the most significant contributions of the CCWHP and the women's movement in general will emerge from the regional associations of women historians. These groups bring together previously isolated women to learn from each other about history and about themselves. The communication thus established and the professional cooperation emerging from these groups may well be the most lasting effect of the women's revolution.

Regional groups range from the long-established and politically sophisticated Berkshire Conference of Women Historians to numerous small groups meeting occasionally to discuss a paper or a project. The State University of New York at Buffalo has a Women's Studies College which offered 45 courses in 1972-73, a good number of which were historical. The University of Indiana has an active women's studies program; Michigan offers graduate work in the field; and California women historians have a West Coast Association almost as large as organizations in the rest of the country added together.

Even the self-congratulations of the Bicentennial have received attention from the Boston 200 Task Force, a group of Boston-area women, mostly historians. They plan a series of lectures and exhibitions to counter anyone's lingering ideas about founding fathers. A catalog of projects and groups would be endless, but one conclusion is clear: organization, activity, and excitement in the study of history belong to the women's movement.

Take for example two recent meetings of the New England Association of Women Historians, a group probably average in size and in industriousness. In November 1973 they met in New Haven to hear from three young women who are all contributors to a forthcoming book on women in Europe. They managed in a brief afternoon to question two assumptions about historical understanding in a way which would undoubtedly offend and instruct many of their male elders. Their joint research covered a lot of ground, from classical Greece to modern Europe, but it came together in suggesting that conventional periodization must be reconsidered if viewed from the perspective of women and, if that is not sufficient, that the historian's implicit faith in perpetual human progress must be rigorously reexamined.

An example should serve to illustrate the challenges they raised. A young specialist in the Renaissance spoke to the obvious but unasked question, "Did women have a renaissance?" Her response was a jolt, for she suggested that the bourgeoisification of Italian society deprived women of power, created a patriarchal culture, and, in general, set women back in their quest for human liberty and autonomy. So what "renaissance" can be considered? What is progress, after all, if the transformation to a modern social order is achieved at the expense of half a population?

Such questions would never have been asked within the context of traditional political and economic history, nor would they emerge in ordinary considerations of intellectual "revolutions." The Renaissance becomes problematic only as a question of social history, and it is precisely that field with which the women's movement has merged to create a wholly new way to regard the human past.

Admittedly, social history in the form of demographic and other quantitative studies became a force in European scholarship two decades ago and migrated to America by the late 1950s. But the study of women's history and the history of the family, an institution with which women are so intimately connected, has provided a conceptual framework for social history research that illuminates much of the data collected by demographic quantifiers. The conjunction of women's studies and social history provides a place for the historian who wants to study the lives of unfamous, unremarkable, and supremely human events—"history from the bottom up" merges with history from the home.

If the November meeting revealed the possibilities of new fields of historical research, the same group of women, meeting in December in Boston, demonstrated the advantages to be gained by teaching innovations generated by the women's movement. In Boston they saw slide shows, collections of visual documentation put together not by large publishing concerns or educational supply houses, but by the women historians who used them—and by their students. Each woman who showed her collection told essentially the same by now familiar story: she had specialized in colonial America, or nineteenth-century France, or whatever, and never learned any more about women's history than her male colleagues. A year before, or two months before, her chairman, besieged by demands from students for a women's history course, looked around at his faculty and found his one woman. No matter that she was as unprepared as the men, she was to teach the women's course.

At that point in her story, groans of recognition ran around the room from women who had shared her predicament. The consequences for all were the same—they hustled bibliographies from old friends, made their own slides, corralled women in other departments to give guest lectures, and slowly discovered the web of friendships and teaching resources, put together rapidly and with little funding, which was developing all across the country. The final result? Team teaching, innovative resources, professional cooperation, cross-disciplinary courses, and joint research projects. In other words, a challenge and rebuke to the individualistic and cut-throat professional style of the male historian in which research, thought, and publication are matters of jealous privacy. A revolution, that is, in academic scholarship.

If you visit the history department of a major university, you will find that the women's history courses are more formal now, that there is a growing number of graduate students trained in the field, and that major research facilities like the Women's History Archives at Berkeley, the Schlesinger Library in Cambridge, and the rediscovered Sophia Smith Collection at Smith are known and used by students at all levels. You will find, too, journals devoted to women's studies like *Feminist Studies* and *Women's Studies*, both with a heavy emphasis on historical material. But you will also find active groups of women graduate students and young faculty members in organized study groups, women active in departmental reform actions, and, most important, women historians talking to each other—about their own history. They form the beginning of a whole new kind of professionalism.

The Feminist Press

By Jean Collins

Florence Howe was teaching women's studies at Goucher College in Towson, Maryland, when courses on women began emerging in colleges and high schools in the 1960s. After having difficulty getting materials to use in her courses, she decided to do something to make information by and about women more accessible. So with 11 other women and 1 man, Howe formed the Feminist Press in Baltimore in 1970. The man was her husband, Paul Lauter, who thought of the name for the organization.

Howe, who describes herself as "the chief cook and bottle washer," has been president of the Feminist Press since its inception. She extended the press to the State University of New York, College of Old Westbury, when she became a professor of humanities there in 1971. According to Howe, the goal of the press has always been to change education through publications, to reach people with stories of women's lives, and to change the books children read in schools and libraries.

The press has grown considerably over the years. At first it was supported entirely by individual contributions and run by volunteers. But several grants from such sources as the Rockefeller Family Fund and the Ford Foundation have made it possible for the press to pay part-time or full-time salaries to 14 of its 19 staff members and to expand publishing ventures and other activities.

The Feminist Press is an educational and publishing corporation, and the only nonprofit, tax-exempt organization concerned with publishing feminist books on a pre-school through adult level. In addition to publishing books such as biographies of women and nonsexist children's books, the press is working on a variety of education projects. These include a clearinghouse on women's studies, an internship in publishing for college students, and an in-service course on sex-role stereotypes for elementary and secondary school teachers.

Verne Moberg, a key full-time staff member, stresses the crucial connection between publishing and education. "People are better editors of educational materials when they're involved in teaching," she says. "They're probably better teachers when they're involved in making books."

There is a busy yet relaxed atmosphere about the complex of Feminist Press offices at SUNY-Old Westbury. The phone rings often; people rush in and out. Books seem to grow out of the walls. "It's more hectic than most offices," Moberg said, "but it's also more cooperative than most. It's not unusual for someone to bring a child to the office when there's a school holiday." Moberg said the press can't properly be described as a collective. "Everyone doesn't take turns doing every job. Specific people are responsible for specific work." The organization is structured in another sense too. The board of the press, consisting of elected members, has the final say on how funds are allocated, which books are published, and what action to take on recommendations from the press committees.

A button on the bulletin board in the main office proclaims, "PUBLISH WOMEN OR PERISH." The Feminist Press is making a significant effort to do the former. Its first book, *The Dragon and the Doctor*, was published in 1971. The dragon in this children's book has a sore tail which is cured by a doctor and her brother, a nurse. Since *The Dragon*, the press has published a total of more than 15 biographies, reprints, children's books, and pamphlets.

The biographies include *Constance de Markievicz* by Jacqueline Van Voris, who is director of an oral history project at Smith College on women's education in the nineteenth century. De Markievicz was an Irish revolutionary who fought for the liberation of Ireland and of women in the early twentieth century. Another Feminist Press biography is *Approaching Simone*, Megan Terry's play about Simone Weil, the French mystic philosopher. *Approaching Simone* won an Obie award for the best play of 1969-70 after only five performances in New York City. One book scheduled for publication soon is *The Life and Times of My Mother and Me* by Madeline Belkin Rose, an oral biography of a Brooklyn immigrant woman who worked in the garment industry in the early part of this century.

The "lost literature" the press has reprinted includes "Life in the Iron Mills," a story by Rebecca Harding Davis which was first published anonymously in the *Atlantic Monthly* in 1861. *Daughter of Earth*, by Agnes Smedley, first published in 1928, is the autobiographical novel of a working-class woman who became a journalist of the Chinese revolution.

Barbara Ehrenreich and Deirdre English, both teachers at Old Westbury, wrote the pamphlets *Witches, Midwives and Nurses: A History of Women Healers* and *Complaints and Disorders: the Sexual Politics of Sickness*. The authors originally published *Witches* themselves, and Ehrenreich said they were expecting a thousand orders at the most. But when a thousand orders a month started pouring in, the Feminist Press agreed to take over the distribution of the book as well as subsequent printings.

The pamphlets, like the reprints, have been widely used in college courses, particularly in American studies, American history, and literature courses. Feminist Press books go to thousands of individuals, bookstores, and libraries, Florence Howe reported. Just a few of the schools that ordered Feminist Press books for the spring 1974 semester included the University of Arkansas, Harvard University, and the University of Illinois Medical School.

Members of the press have always hoped its books would stimulate changes in education. But they didn't anticipate that by 1973 it would be "aiming at *direct* changes in the *institutions* of this country." According to a recent Feminist Press *News/Notes*, this is what the press is seeking to accomplish with a variety of education projects.

At a session of the In-Service Teacher Education Project on sex-role stereotypes, run by the press, Howe talked about why she finds teaching teachers enjoyable and important. "I think the way to change education is to work with teachers," she told the group of approximately 15 elementary and secondary school teachers. "It's slower than handing down books, but it's more meaningful."

The in-service course has been offered several times. It began as a response to a request from some Long Island teachers for help in teaching their own classes and in persuading their school systems to offer in-service courses on sex-role stereotyping. One high school teacher said she was attending the 10-session course at Old Westbury because "I wanted to learn how to prepare students so they won't go out into the world feeling inferior."

The first meeting of a recent course, which several Feminist Press staff members were teaching, opened with each person introducing herself and giving a description of her early education. The majority, including Florence Howe, described themselves as formerly shy, teachers' pets, cupboard-straightener-uppers. Howe told the group that when she had asked men in similar situations to talk about their elementary education, they invariably described themselves in much loftier terms, even though their grades often were poorer than women's at that age.

Other sessions of the course were devoted to such topics as "sex stereotyping in English and social studies texts," "development of nonsexist curriculum units," and "counseling and physical education."

The idea for the Internships in Publishing, another education project, was sparked by the interest of Old Westbury students who would hang around the Feminist Press offices. Six women and one man participated in the program, a course for four credits which began in the spring 1974 semester. The interns met with Feminist Press staff members regularly one hour a week. Then they constructed their own schedule for seven more hours each week. The interns were required to keep a log of their work and the skills they learned in such areas as publishing finance, production, and research.

Christina DiPietro said she became interested in publishing "as the fastest way to reach people." She enrolled in the internship because she wants to learn to be "an efficient tool to accomplish the social aims I'm interested in."

Like many of the interns, Al Curry said he thinks the course could use a little more organization "without having to become regimented." But he thinks this problem can be resolved as the program progresses. Curry, a black man who has worked at the *New York Times* for many years in the communications center, said the availability of the internship helped him decide to go to Old Westbury and complete his college degree.

The Clearinghouse on Women's Studies was the first education project the press developed. Carol Ahlum, a Feminist Press staff member, and Florence Howe organized the clearinghouse to collect information and resources on women's studies at the college level. The clearinghouse now contains the largest body of data on women's studies in the country that the press knows of. Much of that data has been published in several comprehensive guides:

- *The Women's Studies Newsletter*, a 16-page pamphlet, issued quarterly to more than 1,500 subscribers, is the "single most famous publication of the press," Howe said. The *Newsletter* covers news of elementary and high schools and women's studies in colleges.
- *Female Studies VII*, the most recent book in a series, describes some of the more than 2,000 courses and 80 programs in female studies in the United States. One purpose of this guide is to assist women in developing their own courses by providing lists of organizations, bibliographies, and project suggestions.
- *Who's Who and Where in Women's Studies*, published in the summer of 1974, makes available the most complete information on who teaches women's studies and where. It contains listings by individual institutions and departments.

There are too many other education projects to describe them all in detail here. But several of the others focus on elementary education. And the Ford Foundation recently funded the Curriculum Project, for which three staff members have been hired to develop supplementary materials for high school English and social studies courses.

When asked to describe long-range goals she would

like the press to achieve, Moberg laughed, "I'm always glad to get through the day, but don't say that." In a more serious vein, she said she would like the press to take on more feminist oral history, books about feminist learning styles and philosophy, and more third-world subjects. Many other press members also would like to publish more third-world subjects and were pleased recently to receive a grant from the Cummins Engine Foundation for a book on black women. Florence Howe says that she'd like the press to focus on high school in-service and supplementary materials on history and English.

What impact has the Feminist Press had? Statistics tell part of the story. More than 15,000 individuals and institutions are on the mailing list. Orders for thousands of books have been placed. Almost all the books are being printed a second time. Reviews of many of them have appeared in at least a score of newspapers and magazines. Authors are "on the verge" of being able to receive their 50 percent of the income from their books after publishing costs are paid. Approximately 20 letters arrive each day, many from individuals asking for help and support. A typical letter came from a woman in Sunshine, Arkansas, who wanted help in getting Feminist Press books into her local library.

The impact of the press on individuals is easier to measure and perhaps is even more important than statistics. The press has had a pronounced effect on many people closely involved with it, as well as on its audience.

Three women the press influenced are no longer members. They were working with the press as volunteers in its early days. According to Florence Howe, "Learning about feminism caused their confidence to grow and egos to swell so that they began to feel they could do anything!" By the time a grant made it possible to pay them modest salaries, they had all found "fancy jobs."

Paul Lauter said his involvement with the press caused him to learn a "certain level of modesty in teaching situations I hadn't had before. One thing the women's movement has been correctly turned off from is people from an aggressive, white-male background like me. Before, I had used nondirected teaching methods, but I had *imposed* them."

The press also has reached others. A young girl wrote, "I read your book the, 'Firegirl'. It was very good and unusual. Usually a book like that is written about a boy. (I really don't see why)."

A teacher attending the in-service course on sex-role stereotypes said she was taking the course because, like many of the women in her consciousness raising group, she had become "tired of rapping and was ready to do something more active." That's much the same spirit in which the press was created. Now, after more than three years of working on books and education projects, the Feminist Press is helping this woman and others develop the desire and the methods to make the crucial step and translate their awareness into action.

Make Policy, Not Coffee

By Easy Klein

When 50 women, all members of state legislatures, convened at a Pocono Mountain retreat in 1972, one of their high-priority questions was: "Why aren't there more of us?" An outgrowth of that challenge was a pilot course, State Politics and Women Politicians, to encourage and train women who want to enter politics. It was first taught in 1973 at Douglass College of Rutgers University in New Brunswick, New Jersey, and it is expected to become a model for similar programs throughout the country.

The course was designed to supplement theoretical political science programs by bringing undergraduate women into contact with effective political leaders. It was part of the Douglass Visiting Program in Practical Politics. Many college programs feature courses on women in government which rely on visiting politicians as guest lecturers on a one-shot basis. The unique feature of the Douglass program was that the two politicians-in-residence who shared teaching assignments were available to students informally at all times; they lived in a campus dormitory and took their meals at a student cafeteria.

Sixty students enrolled in two sessions of the

course, which met twice a week in an old Victorian house on the campus. There were no textbooks; articles from the *New York Times*, the *Washington Post*, *Ms. Magazine*, and other publications were required reading. It is hoped that the course will be duplicated on other campuses.

"Students rarely come into contact with women in elective office because women have always been underrepresented in public life," says Ruth Mandel, director of the Center for the American Woman and Politics, which sponsored the course. The center is a research unit connected with the Eagleton Institute of Politics at Rutgers.

Ms. Mandel believes that "there is a great deal of value in presenting female role models in all fields in order to give women an idea of the variety of options open to them." One of the options she would like them to explore is state and local politics, where, she says, married women who are not chief breadwinners may have an economic advantage over their male colleagues. Paradoxically, while the women's movement is fighting for equal pay, middle-class women who are supported by their husbands have an advantage in politics because they usually can afford to work for lower salaries. (Salaries for state legislators vary; representatives in New Hampshire receive $200 a year.) While many male legislators must hold two jobs, most women in elective office can devote themselves full time to one. Furthermore, Ms. Mandel points out, women who spend most of their time at home are likely to know more about community problems—from recreation to recycling garbage—than their husbands. By teaching women how to run election campaigns, communicate with their constituents, and deal with party leaders and lobbyists, Ms. Mandel hopes to encourage them to enter public life.

The Douglass visiting program was funded by an

$18,000 grant from the Chase Manhattan Bank and by smaller grants from corporations. It was one of several programs sponsored by the center, whose first major project was the Poconos conference. There, participants agreed that women who want to enter and remain in politics face problems different from those of their male colleagues. Although attitudes are changing, there is still a strong bias among many voters against women running for office. And for those women who come to politics through volunteer organizations, raising campaign funds is more difficult than for men with business connections. If a woman with children is elected to office and has to spend a significant amount of time away from home, she is sometimes criticized for neglecting her family. An analysis of the differences in attitudes and behavior between men and women legislators emerged from the conference as a book entitled *Political Woman*.

Audrey Beck, a representative to the state assembly in Connecticut who attended the Poconos conference, taught the first half of the course at Douglass while the legislature was not in session. A former economics teacher at the University of Connecticut, she was elected in 1968 as the first Democrat in over 50 years to represent her Republican district. When she got to the assembly Ms. Beck found that few women held committee chairmanships and that their influence in party caucuses was limited. She also found separate lunchrooms for men and women, and an overall secondary status for women legislators reflected in committee assignments and nonparticipation in social gatherings where important decisions are often made. Her eight Democratic colleagues joined forces to fight the "backseat syndrome" which tends to keep women out of legislative leadership. In 1972 this female coalition managed to elect Ms. Beck assistant minority leader, a victory that coincided with the first secret ballot in the history of the state Democratic party caucus. The Connecticut legislature is now "among the leaders in according full equality for women on both sides of the aisle," Ms. Beck observes proudly.

"Women have to get in there and take a little mud and get over their fears of stepping on men's toes," she told her students. Ms. Beck maintains a keen interest in education and welfare but refuses to be categorized as a women's issue candidate. She campaigned successfully for income tax reform and has worked on committees dealing with budgets, transportation, industrial modernization, and the status of women in her state.

Louise Conner, who taught the second half of the course, served in the Delaware state senate for eight years until her defeat in 1972. She characterizes herself as a progressive Republican and campaigned in the Senate for fair housing and therapeutic abortion. She sponsored the Equal Rights Amendment prohibiting discrimination based on sex and takes pride in the fact that Delaware was the second state to ratify it.

Ms. Conner predicts an increase in the number of women seeking political power. She feels a responsibility to teach them the political skills they will need to get away from stamp licking and envelope stuffing and into policy making. Ms. Conner learned parliamentary procedure on the job from a woman colleague in the senate who would come up behind her and whisper instructions from Roberts' *Rules of Order* when the going got rough. Although they rarely voted on the same side of an issue, Ms. Conner was grateful for the sisterly coaching in the art of political maneuvering.

In a typical classroom session, Ms. Conner discussed politics and the media—and effectively shattered some student stereotypes of a Republican legislator. She denounced the Nixon Administration for its efforts to intimidate the press and control the free flow of information. "The press and the government are in an adversary role," she told her students, "but they are not enemies. Reporters are professionals with a job to do. They can't be expected to be your advocate when you're in public office."

Many of the Douglass students brought to class a political awareness beyond their years. Roseann Thomas, a student who hopes to study law, was not impressed by the politicians she worked with in New Brunswick community action programs. When she was 18, Ms. Thomas, who is black, ran for election to the board of education in largely white Franklin Township, New Jersey, campaigning on the issue of community control. She lost, but the experience whetted her appetite for political action. "When you're a black woman, you have to fight twice as hard as anyone else. I came to class to learn to be a professional," Ms. Thomas says. She had the confidence of a veteran campaigner, but some of her classmates were embarrassed at the thought of asking for votes. Ms. Beck's candid admission that she too had been reluctant to solicit votes on her own behalf encouraged them in their choice of a political career.

The special problems of women living at the intersection of public and private life provided frequent topics of conversation at the luncheon table where Ms. Conner ate with her students. "You have to be able to keep a lot of things going and not worry about a neat house," she told them. "You don't have to be a superwoman. An ordinary housewife with extra energy and a flexible family can accomplish a great deal on the state and local level." She attributed her own success in combining marriage and a career to an understanding and accommodating husband who shares her interest in politics.

The Visiting Program in Practical Politics was aimed at raising the political consciousness of women. In addition to their teaching assignments, Mss. Conner and Beck lectured and conducted seminars and workshops in a community outreach program in the New Brunswick area. Students who accompanied them to schools, League of Women Voters meetings, and party caucuses gained experience in politics at the grassroots level. Both teachers were also required to submit research projects. Ms. Beck's monograph on state legislative reform—focusing on professionalism, reapportionment, consumerism, and the roles of minorities and women—is available for national distribution through the center. Ms. Conner's research consisted of 10 taped interviews with women politicians—including Jill Ruckelshaus, White House aide in charge of liaison with women's groups, and Pat Schroeder, Democratic Congresswoman from Denver whose husband gave up his law practice to manage her political career. The tapes, which were broadcast by 15 radio stations, are packaged as cassettes and are available to undergraduate classes and women's groups around the country.

Lesbians: The Doors Open

By Cynthia Secor

The seventies are proving a time of quiet renaissance and revolution for the more than twenty million gay people who live and work in the United States. As in other movements for human liberation, the lead is being taken by easily identifiable activists. But theirs is a movement that is still more in the closet than out, despite the publicity given to the gay liberation movement by the media and to the long and turbulent discussions of the lesbian question within the women's movement.

In the late 1960s there began in academic circles—both on campuses and in professional associations—a slow and painful awakening to the presence of women in higher education. Admitting that some of these women are lesbian has been an even slower and more painful process for many—in spite of the polemics and fact-finding of academic feminists. Since higher education opened to women in the 1800s, however, lesbians have been present in force. In 1903 Gertrude Stein wrote matter-of-factly about three young lesbians just out of college, and the following year wrote and subsequently published an account of the romantic lesbian entanglements of faculty and administration at an elite eastern college.

Q.E.D. and *Fernhust*, however, are in effect the exceptions that prove a fundamental rule, for even more so than their counterparts, the male homosexuals, lesbians have remained all but invisible, even to themselves. Until recent years lesbian academic women have shared a lifestyle as quiet and unobtrusive as any in the country. All that is now changing.

In response to the times, the etiquette of invisibility is giving way gradually to the politics of visibility, a trend that is likely to accelerate as gay people organize nationally in advocacy groups. For the past five years, the lesbian issue on campus has been a feminist issue—political in that sexual preference is, like free day care and abortion, a controversial but legitimate issue to raise. Moreover, those on campus who have chosen to identify themselves as lesbians have been, almost without exception, feminist activists. Until recently, reformist gay activism had not affected the campus directly. Daughters of Bilitis and the Mattachine Society, for instance, had student and academic members, but their chapters were never campus-based, and they did not directly affect professional matters or curricular materials. They functioned in effect as urban-based local groups.

But the year 1973 marked the formation of the first truly national advocacy groups that want specifically to affect campus life: the Gay Academic Union (GAU) with its highly successful national convention; the National Gay Task Force (NGTF), headed by Dr. Howard J. Brown, the former Commissioner of Health of New York City; and caucuses in the Modern Language Association (MLA), the American Historical Association (AHA), and the American Anthropological Association (AAA). The GAU's statement of purpose describes well these new groups' perspective: "We committed ourselves to actively oppose sexism in the educational system and all forms of discrimination against women and gay people, to support individual academics in the process of coming out, to combat myths about gayness, and to promote new kinds of scholarship and the teaching of gay studies." Their first national conference, the Universities and the Gay Experience, attracted 325 participants from 18 states representing 65 colleges and universities.

Work in the professional associations is likely to proceed along several lines. The 1973 annual business meeting of the AHA was presented with a resolution against "homophobia in the profession." In 1974 the Berkshire Conference, a gathering of women historians, had a panel on bisexuality and homosexuality. The gay anthropologists resolved to have a symposium on homosexuality at their meeting in Mexico City, where papers on "The Woman-Identified Woman" by a woman anthropologist and on "Gay Slang/Gay Culture" by linguist Julia Stanley were presented. The MLA's caucus has been granted the status of an associated meeting. In addition to their business meeting they are sponsoring workshops on the homosexual in the teaching profession, teaching gay literature, lesbians and literature, and a major open forum for Christopher Isherwood to make a personal statement about his life as a novelist who is also gay.

These organizations and caucuses have, along with gay advocacy books from the major presses, created a social climate in which lesbians and male homosexuals are beginning to feel safe to organize—if not on their own campuses, where the threat of reprisals from administrators and departmental colleagues is still, for the most part, too heavy to ignore, then at least in their professional associations. The national organizational scope, paradoxically, affords a greater measure of personal privacy and helps "legitimize" the concerns of the gay professional for the right to teach and choose curricular materials without harassment.

The professional and curricular interests of the lesbian professional are likely to develop locally very much in conjunction with women's studies, if only because the women working in these national organizations are teaching women's studies courses on their own campuses. Because it is impossible to foresee lesbian studies developing apart from women's studies, their fate locally probably depends on the ease with which particular feminists have been able to deal with lesbianism as a theoretical issue and as an active presence. The role of the lesbian in such local groups is complex because she is perceived both as victim and societal scapegoat, and as leader and member of an elite. Many fear her as outlaw, as felon, and as a living embodiment of evil. These attitudes, though outmoded, are real; and though our society is becoming more accepting of sexuality in its various forms, feminism as a social movement puts this acceptance to the test, for within the women's movement numerous lesbians occupy positions of leadership. And as the movement grows, their power and authority will grow.

The common pattern has been to include lesbian materials in courses of general interest, but a number of specifically lesbian courses have been taught for credit at, for example, Richmond College of the City University of New York (CUNY), San Francisco State, New York University (NYU), and Kent State. Elsewhere, as at the University of Pennsylvania and the Everywoman's Center of the University of Massachusetts at Amherst, these courses are offered through a free university or women's center.

The women on campus today who publicly identify

themselves as lesbians are not victimized women suing for acceptance. Rather, they are faculty women like Dolores Noll at Kent State or Sally Gearhart at San Francisco State who are helping to build feminist and gay movements. They are graduate students like J. Lee Lehman, director of the National Gay Student Center, a project of the United States National Student Association. They are radical lesbian separatists, like those at Penn who live communally off-campus and work with community lesbians to set up services such as hotlines, coffeehouses, and rap groups for older women in the process of coming out. They are the students who get student activities money to bring Jill Johnston to campus, who petition to read Gertrude Stein in their literature courses, and who discuss in American history courses the female companions of Frances Willard and Jane Addams. At Case Western Reserve University they hold a lesbian feminist conference. They converge at Sacramento State to protest the absence of lesbian perspectives in a women's studies conference.

The idea of the lesbian as a political person has gained such rapid acceptance that in a recent issue of *Ms.* a journalist refused to identify Alice B. Toklas and Gertrude Stein as lesbians on the rather dubious grounds that these lifelong companions and lovers had been too apolitical to be lesbians as the term is currently understood. There are those who would say things have gone too far when the most famous lesbians since Sappho are in danger of being stripped of their identity—just as the literary and scholarly establishments seem at last ready to deal with it seriously and maturely.

The fact remains, however, that the activists are having an impact out of proportion to their number, and that in the process they are redefining what it means to be a lesbian. Their number is increasing, as many feminists, for political reasons, choose to take on the label "lesbian" and as closet academics take courage from the activists' example and tangible success. But it is still not at all clear that the majority of closet lesbians will come out in the name of their own liberation, so that the activist minority creates a distorted public image of lesbian goals, opinions, and lifestyles. The vast majority of lesbians do not think of their lifestyles as political, and they are still far from being open with family, co-workers, or other students. They are certainly not radical separatists and often steer clear of women's centers and women's studies programs where there is an overt lesbian presence. Their long habit of silence and invisibility is not easily broken. And reasonably enough, for they usually know at first hand of lesbians who have been blackmailed, fired, or otherwise harassed simply for daring to exist.

One of the harsh ironies of lesbian academic life today is that the blackmail threat from a rejected lover or a malicious co-worker has been joined by political blackmail. Traditionally, one feared being called up before a dean or college president to answer charges. Now one fears being challenged in an open meeting as Kate Millett was at Columbia, since collectivists and radicals often feel justified in forcing a lesbian faculty person or administrator into the open. Similarly, closet lesbians sometimes try to obstruct feminist or gay projects as a way of diverting "suspicion" from themselves.

Much work of the most conventional kind remains to be done. Hopefully the existence of GAU and NGTF and their commitment to lesbian concerns will make it easier for Women's Equity Action League (WEAL) and Committee W of the AAUP to face up to the patterns of discrimination and instances of individual injustice their lesbian members experience. At the moment the National Organization for Women is the only national feminist organization that voices as a matter of established policy the concerns of its lesbian members. Very hopeful, however, is the case reported by the Association of American Colleges' Project on the Status and Education of Women in their December 1973 newsletter: "Susan Brown, supported by the National Education Association, has filed suit for reinstatement, back salary and $100,000 in damages against Ames College (Greeley, Colorado) alleging that she was denied a second-year contract for presenting a panel on lesbianism in her 'Psychology of Women' course."

Affirmative action offers a hope of real progress. While it is unlikely that lesbians in the near future will push for preferential hiring, it is centrally important that the persons charged with administering grievance mechanisms understand that lesbians are particularly vulnerable to the backlash against women and are very often unable to put forward the complete details of their cases. Single women, often mistakenly identified as lesbians, are also vulnerable. Consider the dilemma of a single woman on the west coast up for promotion. A member of the department described her in an unfavorable letter of evaluation as his department's Jill Johnston. Was one to assume she is English? Creative? A feminist? A lesbian? A troublemaker? Depending on one's point of view the comment is humorous, slanderous, or discriminatory.

Local academic women's rights groups and their state or regional equivalents should familiarize themselves with state laws, court cases, professional licensing criteria, the ethical codes of their professions, and criminal codes that affect lesbians. In all but seven states acting sexually on one's homosexual feelings is punishable by imprisonment. Though such sanctions are seldom invoked, they dramatize the legal status of gay people, their vulnerability to blackmail, and the degree to which they remain the scapegoats of our puritanical habits of mind. Academic women's rights groups must come to see that lesbian students, staff, administration, and faculty have legal and employment problems over and above those faced by other women. Faculty and administration, for instance, would be directly affected by passage of legislation such as House Bill 1776, under consideration in fall 1974 in the Missouri House of Representatives. This bill would officially brand homosexuality as a "disease" and would require gay persons to report themselves to the state Division of Health.

It is extremely important that those who counsel pre-law and pre-med students understand that lesbian students may later face hostile licensing boards and prejudicial codes of ethical conduct. And the Acanfora case reminds us just how risky it is for a student to be openly gay if she hopes later to be employed as a public school teacher. Joseph Acanfora III was transferred out of his Maryland classroom when school officials discovered he was gay. The Supreme Court is being asked to review the Fourth Circuit Court of Appeals decision refusing to order his reinstatement because he had failed to inform school officials of his membership in a gay student organization, Homophiles, at Penn State. According to the NGTF newsletter, school officials admitted at the trial that he would not have been hired if he had disclosed his membership in the group because it was the policy of the Montgomery County, Maryland, school board not to hire known homosexuals.

It is still a rare college or university that has elaborate counseling and informational facilities such as those at the University of Michigan, where two permanent salaried employees, a lesbian and a male homosexual, work in the Office of Special Services and Programs as Gay Advocates.

The work that remains to be done is not the work of a season or two, but it is well and safely begun. Lesbian activists can afford to be optimistic. For most in higher education, the seventies now seem a period of tightening belts and retrenchment, but history is likely to record that for lesbians, as for other women, it was the beginning of an era of doors opening, never to be closed again.

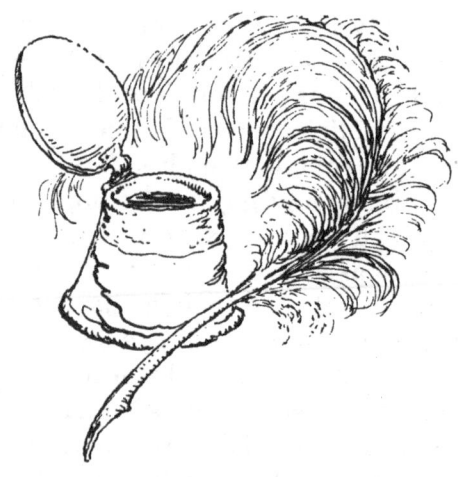

Learning the Hard Way

By Celia Morris

People write such nonsense about higher education. So often they talk as though it were a matter of certain courses or majors, of an occasional intellectual challenge—of the steady accumulation of knowledge and skills that will provide the basis of a life fruitfully lived. But formulations with so little human resonance have to be wrong. My own experience of university life was in the fifties—unlike the sixties, to be sure, but I suspect very much like times before and after. And that experience seems to me now both inspiring and destructive. Nor can I see how, given the time and place and person, it could have been significantly other.

I went to the University of Texas because it was at once the easiest and most challenging thing to do. I was from Houston, and my father wanted me to go to Rice Institute and live at home. Rice was a small college and perhaps the most distinguished one in Texas, and I knew the schooling I'd get there was the best available. But Houston was suffocating, and staying home seemed unventuresome. Several friends were going to ladies' schools in Virginia, but that wasn't my style—nor did I aspire to it. A counselor faintly suggested Radcliffe, but Radcliffe and the East might as well have been mythical. (I'd only been in two other states, and one of them was Oklahoma—just to say I'd been.)

I wanted to go to Austin and could do so without breaking irrevocably from my past. I'd gone several times for football games and parties, and I loved its textures, loved the gentle hills and limestone facades and red tile roofs. The life I saw was exuberant and charmed. I reasoned, perhaps correctly, that if you could learn to live at a big state university, you could survive anything. And I relished the challenge.

So early in September of 1953, my mother left me on the stairway of the murky old Littlefield dormitory that had housed a thousand score nervously hopeful freshmen. The rooms were small: the two beds had to be folded into the closet before anyone could walk about. But who cared for comfort? Outside my window was a glorious magnolia tree; through its leaves I saw the great Tower half a mile away. And freedom was the grandest thing I'd known.

It does, I think, no untoward violence to fact to reconstruct my university days neatly by putting on one side a liberal arts program called Plan II and on the other sorority life, for then one must puzzle out what each had to do with the other. Scarred by the Depression and dubious of things impractical, my mother wanted me to major in physical education or home economics. But common sense struck me as colossally boring. Plan II was a special program that took about 150 students a year, promised them the best professors and most searching courses, cut through departmental red tape, and appealed as both exclusive and rigorous. It offered what seemed the authority of a great tradition and, academically, an escape from the anonymity of a big campus. I hadn't heard of Matthew Arnold, but I'm sure I vaguely assumed that Plan II would make me know the best that had been thought and written—a prospect that seemed wondrously pleasant.

Sorority rush was a more tangible side of Texas, introducing, as it did, the daughters of the respectable and the reasonably affluent. My background was modest, but I was what the sociologists call—horrid term—upwardly mobile. I'd been a star of sorts in high school and could be expected to fit comfortably into the Texas version of upper-middle-class life. The young women I met were healthy and often handsome, most of them effervescent in the style of the day, all of them well-groomed and attractively dressed. They shared the exuberance of favored young people beginning adult life and seemed to manage with as little personal vindictiveness and ill-temper as any group I've seen.

At the time I had no reason to imagine that I'd spend my life anywhere but in Texas. And it was an unstated assumption that the fraternity boys at the university, especially those at the law school, would go on to run the state: to be the executives of its major corporations and whatever. These men, and the less favored ones who aspired to be like them, would accede to power when their time came, and their wives would come precisely from the group I was meeting now. If I were so sensible as to enjoy that life, to admire and want to be part of what makes Texas work, some of these women—and others like them from, say, Southern Methodist University or Texas Tech—would be lifetime companions. I suspected then and later knew that our lives would be similar: we'd swim, water-ski, play tennis, or golf. We'd give and go to parties in the same style. And if we chose occasionally to leave the comforts of exceedingly comfortable homes, we'd probably do the kind of civic work responsible women did in Texas: we'd be volunteers in hospitals, we'd direct charity balls, we'd organize state campaigns for funds to combat multiple sclerosis, if we were lucky we'd make the

Junior League, and if we were superlatively good at it we'd become grand dames.

When the hysterias of rush were over, my first ugly jolt came. My roommate, a gentle, small-town girl, had been rejected by the two sororities she wanted most. I'd known it could happen, but knowing beforehand has never quite steadied me for the hurt that can come. Her misery was the first false note in the merry tune that was to play another couple of years for me. But since I could do nothing to help, and after the first debilitating sympathy passed, I joined in the games and rituals and sentimentalities that make up the sorority whirl.

Academic life, from the beginning, was less ambivalent. Most marvelous by far was a course in world literature taught by an elegant Byron scholar named Willis Pratt. My father, improbably enough, had been able to recite, in Middle English, the first 20 lines of the Prologue to the *Canterbury Tales*, and I discovered with astonished delight that I could learn to do it too. Since I had an ingrained belief that you had to work terribly hard for any pleasure worth having and for quite a few that weren't as well, it seemed only fitting to have to struggle with language alien to my ears. And the effort rewarded me with a sense that I'd finally found a world that could never disappoint. The power of art— of language and sound and rhythm—had finally touched me, and perhaps the lateness of the touch made it all the more indelible. So a girl from Houston, Texas, who hadn't really known that history existed, launched a belated, inchoate, and apparently endless quest into the past in search of beauty.

I slept only four or five hours a night, usually from midnight to dawn. Long before many others got up for breakfast and classes, I'd be sitting at my desk gazing out, when the Puritan ethic permitted, on the great Tower that dominated the campus. It housed part of the library, some of our classrooms, and the administrative offices that organized our lives. It was 15 years later when Charles Whitman took a cache of guns to the top and, with demented precision, murdered 19 people. His act so corrodes my memory of what that ungainly structure meant that it's hard to recover its early beneficent power over my imagination. But I think it did what a symbol does: it summarized in itself a whole place, a complex of activities, and the variety of emotions that place and those things call forth. It was the clean satisfaction of work worth doing: solid, permanent work. It was the excitement and power of knowledge. It was the exhilaration of freedom.

They were very wonderful things to me then, and I suppose they remain so. But in 1953 I didn't know how hard it was to recognize work that mattered. I didn't know how hard it was to be permitted by circumstance and the powers that be to do that work. I didn't know how much there was in all those books that was dross, how much was wrong, how much dubious, how much vicious, how much plain bullshit. No: then it all seemed unified and attainable if one only cared enough to want it and worked single-mindedly enough to deserve it. In the pristine clarity of an early Texas morning, I knew little of contradictory purposes, confused values, fear, and self-destructiveness—all of which would come in time.

And so I was absurdly busy. I believed that one needed to be a good citizen and accepted the prevailing definitions of what that meant: serving on committees for elections and benefits and parties and so on. I dated lots of clever and not-so-clever young men. And I believed the people who said I should study two hours outside for every hour spent in class. Anna Hiss, Alger's sister, was the head of the women's physical education department. A gaunt, impressive lady who was most decisively from New England, she was very much respected on the campus. Strange as it may seem, one couldn't imagine, in her presence, that decent people could fail. There was simply the ramrod back, the sharp blue eyes, and a firmness of purpose utterly undaunted. And she made out a chart that was to help me live sensibly and constructively. It left very little time uncommitted to classes or study or campus activities. There didn't seem an hour left over for relishing one's own humanity or, more to the point, discovering whether one had any. That chart daunted me so that I cried, but not in front of Miss Hiss. And such was the power of her example that for a long time I followed it closely more often than not.

With luck, I came to know the excitement that comes from thinking with others. Five young women would gather in the evenings in one of the dim stuccoed rooms we managed to make into home. We were from Amarillo, Houston, and San Antonio and were typical enough products of our time and our region. In those days we were said to be "well-rounded" or to have "leadership potential." We'd done the things our culture gave the prizes for: we'd been cheerleaders, editors, school and club officers; we were good at swimming or archery or tennis. We'd dated frequently though antiseptically, gone to coke parties, giggled in corridors, cared about clothes. Had anyone said we were spoiled we'd have been surprised and then perhaps indignant. We did more than our share. We had, simply, no idea what extremes of wealth and poverty or racial hatred were—or what their existence had to do with our lives. Nor was official Texas or its university inclined to teach us. We were straight middle class; we lived with blinders the fifties clamped on especially hard to block out the disturbing sights of misery or injustice.

Nor were we encouraged—I'm even tempted to say allowed—to recognize and acknowledge our own private pain. Our pooled experience included death, divorce, and family hatred, but if we mentioned such things we did so quickly. Brightness was all. If we couldn't be cheerful we could at least manage a genial stoicism. Texas in the fifties tended to equate self-consciousness with self-indulgence and to damn them both as sins. None of us had genius or a talent that would seize and organize us with its demands. Untouched by mysticism or radical doubt, we were intelligent, credulous, hopelessly straight.

We'd all done well in school before, but this was the first time our imaginations had been really stirred and excited. We'd fire questions at each other, wend our way through tortuous explanations and genealogies, make up the most outlandish mnemonic devices, and share the kind of simple mental labor that seemed the necessary underpinnings of a decent understanding of ourselves and history. At last I'd discovered young women who wanted to think and to talk about something more impersonal and more important than the standard girls' topics, who had the kind of formless hunger I did. We weren't, to be sure, very good at it: however sympathetic, an observer steeped in history or literature would have been startled at our ignorance and naiveté. But then we hadn't been brought up to believe the intellectual quest necessary to anyone's life, much less to a woman's, and we didn't have the tools.

In our studiousness we were rather suspect to others. Still, we hadn't expected to be scholars, weren't interested in becoming scholarly and probably weren't temperamentally suited for it. In fact, we didn't even know what scholarship meant. It isn't fashionable these days to admit it, nor was it then—but I think most of us were like Dorothea, George Eliot's heroine in *Middlemarch*. We wanted to prepare ourselves for responsible lives in touch with the things that had moved people in Western culture for centuries. Long after, we would realize that Texas had probably offered more choice for women but with less sureness than provincial nineteenth century England had. And, except for an occasional enclave, it was even more remote than Dorothea's small town in the midlands from whatever we mean when we refer to high culture.

Several of us were drawn to groups that were trying to celebrate the meaning Christianity had for them. Strangely enough in a culture where official Christianity is very powerful indeed, only one of us had been brought up so entirely in a church's sway that she never seriously doubted its message. We all were, in varying degrees, contemptuous of the social hypocrisy that frequently passed for Christianity. But a few people in Austin had a goodness and luminosity that testified to their faith and made their way seem best. One of those was the secretary of the YM-YWCA, an old man whose name was Block Smith. He'd gone to Siberia when he was young, then come back to Texas and set up the Y, inviting people to speak at his place off campus when they were anathema to the official university and as often as not banned by it. I thought of him as a primitive Christian: a spare man untempted by pomp and indifferent to circumstance. He had the clarity of soul people have in mind when they speak of humility and the courage to fight the good fights there—especially McCarthyism and racism—in his own gently humorous but implacable way. Leaving a meeting once with a professor renowned for pleasing everyone, he told him, "Dwight, next time we go to one of those, I'm gonna give you a liver pill so you'll stand up for something."

A beautiful man—Block Smith—whose life had been rich and good, and though he didn't encourage people to be his disciples, I desperately wanted to be one. I'd tried for years to be a Christian, had got myself baptized and confirmed in the Episcopal Church when I was 15. But I was plagued with disbelief. Under the supervision of a supposedly outstanding campus minister, I wrote an 80-page junior tutorial paper called "A Modern American in Search of a Religious Faith." It makes painful reading today. The text is full of need and the desire to believe; the problems are stated clearly. But the bibliography is shockingly bad: it includes Anne Morrow Lindbergh, Walter Lippman, and Elton Trueblood rather than Niebuhr, Tillich, or William James. And I actually concluded that studying theology was the way to submit at last to the faith. Nevertheless, I was either too daunted by the prose of the Fathers or too sensible to believe that it would work. At about the same time I discovered *The Brothers Karamazov*, and Ivan's reasons for disbelief convinced me, though I knew paradoxically they hadn't convinced Dostoevski. For me it would remain eternally true that the mother could forgive God for her own pain but not for her child's. But Block loved me anyway. That, I still believe, is what the real Christians do.

Meanwhile the five of us learned Hannibal's battle plans and the layout of the Roman forum. We learned what the authorities apparently consider the reasons for the fall of the Roman Empire. (On the exam I forgot to mention the barbarian invasions, but I made a 96 nonetheless.) We sat at the feet of a man who used the Socratic method with stunning mastery. We read *Antigone, Madame Bovary*, and *Moby Dick*. We dissected a pig, though the formaldehyde made me vaguely ill and I was more or less rescued by a lab partner who wanted to be a mortician and did most of the work. I learned that it was incorrect to say "more or less": "Miss Buchan, it is either more *or* less."

Several of us took a year's course in physics, where the vagaries of my own response to academic life became surprisingly clear. Somewhere between the first and second semesters I shed the conviction that to miss an A was to languish in Purgatory. The first semester I had a crush on the professor and did splendidly. The teacher the second time round was different, and the class met at 2 in the afternoon. Though I regularly fell asleep, I went into the final with a 98 average. But I hadn't studied for weeks, and it seemed like an IQ quiz for which you weren't supposed to know the answers. I doubtless failed, but the professor gave me a B in the course, thinking perhaps I'd had an aberrant day and surely not wanting the trouble of writing another exam.

We memorized the titles of the people and committees that officially run Texas, but we never heard how big money controls the state. We learned something about the inventions that made possible the Industrial Revolution, but we heard little about its human toll. (Texas culture and most Texans we knew would have approved of the Manchester industrialist's response to one who saw the squalor: "But Mr. Engels, a great deal of money is made here.") None of us read Marx at all, much less carefully. We read *Oedipus Rex*, but so far as we knew Freud was a dirty old man.

Shirley and I became enamoured of great art and took a year's course in the Italian Renaissance and then a semester in the Baroque. We'd walk around Austin learning, each semester, about 300 works of art, who'd done them and when, how they were best described, what the historians thought of them. I did an elaborately thorough paper on Gian Lorenzo Bernini's small group statuary but was startled a few years ago to discover in Rome that not only didn't I remember most of those statues—I didn't even like them. We still delight, Shirley and I, in wandering through galleries and have a splendid time whenever we have the chance. But either of us is lucky to get half the painters right—even the ones we once knew so well.

The five of us liked each other, despite occasional mute hostilities. Though our values and interests were incoherent, such as they were they drew us together and weaned us away from whatever allegiances we'd had to our sororities and the extension of them we knew would be our lot if we married the expected people and did the expected things. Carol and I went to Europe between our sophomore and junior years for a reverent, exhilarating, often hilarious adventure. And the same summer several good friends and sorority sisters went to Hawaii. The roads had diverged, and for me there would be no returning. The Hawaii people went on to make their debuts around the state and to become ever more committed to the patterns of a remarkably comfortable life. I came more and more to disdain upper-middle-class Texas: it seemed inane at best, haughty and hypocritical at worst. I stopped going to football games—a staple of the place—after I asked in distraction for the third Saturday in a row which team was Arkansas.

Feelings were badly hurt all round: these were real and once dear people whom I was beginning to reject, and I seemed, even to myself, to be rejecting them for an abstraction. (What indeed was Hecuba to me or me to Hecuba that I should spurn comfort, kindness, and familiarity for her?) Our education had, it seemed, worked at cross-purposes with Texas life, and I was becoming increasingly baffled about what my interest in great books or great art could ever mean in daily terms. I began to suspect I'd indulged in illusion when I hoped to live "a responsible life in touch with the things that had moved people in Western culture for centuries."

The great books were, as often as not, about despair and thwarted purposes, about tragic misperceptions. And people I knew in Texas seemed to find it ill-mannered to recognize, much less to understand, that the economy of the universe might not favor the earnest, the well-mannered, and the kind. Personal failure, for the most part, was chalked up to personal weakness. The charity the upper middle class dutifully dispensed was very different, I'd discovered, from Charity. Apparently Grace would not come, and grace, which might be accessible, was clearly something other than what passed there for style. In short, I found imagining the good life in specific terms far more difficult than I'd suspected a few years earlier. I was inching crabwise away from most of what I'd known.

Even the five of us started losing our cohesiveness. We continued to do well: we all graduated magna or summa cum laude and Phi Beta Kappa. We won, among us, a good many prizes the campus offered. But we found it harder to sustain what people in the sixties called a sense of relevance. Though I still believe it was the best undergraduate education Texas then could give, the ultimate incoherence of our curriculum took its toll. Dissecting a cow's eye one hour and discussing *Don Juan* the next leaves one with a sense of some confusion. The bits and pieces we so laboriously memorized faded quickly except for the ones about which we cared passionately. We lost our early readiness to believe we should learn whatever we were told to learn, but no organizing principle took the place of dutifulness.

Three of the women met the men they live with still. Whether their energies focused or they subconsciously withdrew to ponder so profound a change in their lives, they had time for only necessary work with those of us whose immediate futures were still unclear. In fact, all of us married within a year after we graduated. Though we'd been relatively independent compared to our peers, we didn't find the strength to fight cultural biases so deeply ingrained: to fail to marry early was to violate life's inherent phasing. When I seemed neglectful of my proper function in life, the professor who then had most power over my imagination even said scornfully: "What's wrong with you? Aren't you ever going to fall in love?" Some of us waited until our wedding nights to sleep with the men we married, and some did not. But none of us had ever slept with anyone else. All of us, when we married, left Texas.

Of course it's easy to scoff at our confusion. It's easy to say we were spoiled middle-class women who needn't think seriously about working and who wanted to dispense mercy, justice, and charm from the depths of a Mies van der Rohe chair. It's humiliating to realize how nearly right those people were who thought we were prigs, who opted for sex, who sneered at the goodie-goodies so dumb as to believe in study and something called campus service. There's some truth in every charge against us.

More important, there's the unquestionable fact that we gained very much from our four or five years in Austin. The University of Texas was by no means upper middle class, and we met there many kinds of people we'd never known before—Texas Jews, mid-East Arabs, even an occasional black. In my senior year of high school we hadn't had a civics textbook since the school board banned the one proposed because it included a reference to "one world." A man from the American Civil Liberties Union was refused the right to speak in my junior high school auditorium, and conventional wisdom had it that the NAACP was a Communist front. The university changed my sense of all that. To my father's unrelenting dismay, the University of Texas slowly and insidiously made me into a democrat.

In Austin we made the discovery, more important still, of permanent friendship. Three of those original five remain the closest friends—despite distance and to the death. And the university introduced us to very wonderful things, things we love still and will continue to do. We'd all argue, for example, that we'd rather be able to read W.H. Auden and Louise Bogan with pleasure than to think Rod McKuen is grand. We'd rather not believe that legislation opens the door to socialism if it requires trucks carrying migrant laborers to have workable windshield wipers and to make rest stops every five hours or so. I'm ready to believe I'm better off living where my son isn't damned as peculiar because he doesn't play Little League baseball or go to Sunday school. And leaving has been more *interesting* than staying would have been.

Still, I'm struck by a powerful conviction of waste —the waste of energy and time and unstated hope. We wanted coherence; we wanted to be useful without being martyrs. And instead, some of us began to develop the tragic sense of life. Without having discovered what kind of work we could do that was truly worth doing, we all left Texas and only two have returned. Our awards and honors blinded us to our ignorance, and for that ignorance, sexual and otherwise, some of us paid in blasted marriages and anguished years.

Romanticize Texas and you're sillier than we were then. But the sky is more beautiful there—and the contorted forms of the live oak, the gray, almost monumental cacti, the cold water pools, the rhythms and tones of goodness as I knew it first. Only a Pollyanna can see such loss as pure gain—or the need to start over in other places, to begin a provisional, rootless, tone-deaf life. It wouldn't help to fake at Pollyanna and say, Isn't it lucky that we learned to read *Othello*. I'm not convinced that learning to read *Othello* matters crucially, though I believe that learning to recognize the difference between deception and loyalty does. But clear-mindedness and self-consciousness aren't qualities that a hard-playing, sun-loving, money culture encourages. Ambivalence became—and remains—a way of being in the world.

Unemployed! An Academic Woman's Saga

By Elaine B. Hopkins

After five years of university teaching I find myself unemployed, with no prospect of finding an academic job. My position wasn't phased out—others are teaching my courses this year. And I am not incompetent: my chairman recommended me as a hard worker and an excellent teacher. In fact, I've done it all: served on committees, addressed peace rallies, organized a women's liberation front, advised a sorority, delivered a paper at a convention, published a few obscure articles, even had a baby—but it wasn't enough. Like most women who've entered the portals of academe, I didn't survive the gauntlet that leads to a permanent niche in the ivory tower. My university didn't say in writing that it wanted 82 percent of its teaching faculty to be male. It simply devised policies which, given the pattern of women's participation in higher education, guarantee that only token numbers of women will stay there long. Then it rationalized those policies by elaborate justifications which would be the envy of an oriental bureaucracy. I call it the "vanishing Indian" syndrome. Everyone is sorry that the poor Indian (or woman) is disappearing, but after all, he (she) stands in the way of "progress," which is "good," though it squashes everything in its path.

If all this sounds too harsh and cynical, read on and then judge for yourself.

My story really begins in 1956. I was the bright, pretty, only child of lower-middle-class parents, and I understood that social mobility for a woman meant capturing an upwardly mobile husband. I graduated from a public high school and entered college for the sole purpose of making myself into a presentable wife for my fiance, who planned to become an attorney. But college genuinely awakened me. I loved it; I was hooked. My parents turned pale when I told them I wanted to stay long enough to graduate. But they scraped together some of the money, I won some scholarships, and by 1960 I was a 20-year-old BA. Soon I was married (to a different guy), then pregnant, a mother, a kindergarten teacher (with no training), and a Navy wife. My husband decided that flying planes for the Navy was scary when it wasn't boring, so he entered graduate school. Though my undergraduate grades had been higher than his, I was terrified of such an adventure and found a job as a secretary instead. Two years later the academic world wasn't so strange, and at 26 I finally found the courage to begin graduate work. By the time my husband received his PhD, I had earned my MA.

He secured a position at an "emerging" Midwestern university; I wrote hoping for a part-time position, only to be told that there was a nepotism rule against employing faculty wives—a rule that could, however, be waived in an "emergency." I signed a temporary contract the day before the fall quarter started and began teaching four sections of freshman composition. I loved it. I was good at it. And I began to wonder how I could get tenure and turn my job into a career.

Thrusting skyward from rich Midwestern corn fields, Western Illinois University (WIU) in Macomb was an obscure teachers college until the mid-1950s, when the Illinois legislature changed its name and funded its expansion to a university of 14,000 students. But its growing pains appeared to be over when my husband and I were hired in 1968. A new, progressive president abolished the nepotism policy, and in 1969 I signed a regular, probationary contract, taught a sophomore course and got pregnant. Our second child was born in July 1970. I never missed a day of work, which was fortunate since there was no maternity leave for pregnant faculty with less than three years of service. Nor was there a day care center, but we luckily found a wonderful baby-sitter. Then on December 1, 1970, a disaster: I, along with every instructor in English in his third year of teaching or later, received a letter from the provost notifying me that my contract would not be renewed for the following year. No reasons were given. We were thanked and dismissed.

The grapevine soon told us that the reasons behind our dismissals were subtle and complicated. WIU wanted to continue "emerging" by establishing a doctor of arts program—which ultimately never got off the ground—and it needed our positions to hire PhDs. Then, too, some of the instructors were outspoken on issues ranging from the Vietnam War to departmental priorities; the tenured faculty wouldn't weep to see them depart. Also, the instructors outnumbered the senior faculty, who needlessly feared they might organize and start running the department. Of course, many of the instructors were women and therefore dispensable.

Officially we were told, though not in writing, that we had not made "adequate progress" toward our doctorates. The faculty and Board of Governors' handbooks stated that a faculty member must earn

30 semester hours beyond his or her master's within six years to be eligible for tenure, but nothing was said about *when* these hours must be earned. The administration claimed that we should have been attending graduate school during summers, though no one had so advised us.

At this point we were temporarily saved by AAUP guidelines that say faculty in their third year of teaching must receive one year's notice if they are not being rehired. So the administration offered us terminal contracts for 1971-72. Since a terminal contract was better than no contract, I signed it and spent the summer in graduate school. When the fall quarter began, I and the few who remained again appealed through all the channels for a more equitable deal. After the dean refused to hear the case on the grounds that it had been permanently settled, my colleagues gave up and made plans to leave. But as a faculty wife with two children, I was stuck in Macomb, and with nothing to lose I pushed my appeal all the way to the provost. In late May he made a concession: if the English department approved my doctoral program, I could be retained to teach lower division courses for one more year.

My head was spinning. I kept asking what my graduate program had to do with my ability to teach composition, and I was told that I couldn't be tenured as a lower division teacher. Everyone knew that English teachers hated to teach composition; all the good schools were abolishing it as a required course and so would WIU some day; then what would they do with me if I had tenure? No one could be tenured without a doctoral field useful to the department; furthermore, no one was going to get tenure without a "terminal degree" anyway, which in English meant the PhD.

So summer came. I went to graduate school again, sent the department my proposed program for the doctorate, and of course they didn't approve it. Teaching composition for four years had stimulated my interest, and I had found a very respectable doctoral program which would emphasize the teaching of composition and literature. "What this world needs is not another expert in literature but people skilled in teaching writing and teaching others to teach it," I naively thought. But my department disagreed. It wanted PhDs in literature and had no use for anyone else, especially someone tainted with education courses. The letter argued that I would have nothing to teach after I finished my doctorate, so I certainly couldn't be rehired. At this point I was desperate. With the local American Federation of Teachers chapter twisting his arm, the provost agreed that my doctoral program really wouldn't destroy my ability to teach lower division courses. I signed a one-year contract. And a week before the fall quarter began, I was assigned to teach an advanced course, Composition for Teachers.

So as the quarter started, I began to realize that the facts in my case just didn't add up. I was a competent faculty member, but I was losing my job. My department didn't want me, but it needed me. And I started wondering if what was happening to me could be considered discriminatory. Always the dutiful scholar, I headed for the library, and as I researched the role and place of women in higher education, I began to see that I was indeed a woman caught up in an alien world. For academe is a place created and controlled by men—a place that rewards those who do what men have been trained to believe is valuable, within the time men think is adequate. Having originated in the medieval monastery, the modern university is a world of credentialed scholars competing for status. It is ordered by male values and priorities and most easily accommodates those whose life styles and sex roles give them the time and energy to acquire credentials, research, publish, and administer the activities of subordinates. Most women in academe either do not accept such a value system (they spend most of their time teaching) or cannot conform to it—which should not surprise us when we consider that women are socialized from the cradle to assume "appropriate" sex roles. By the time they begin college teaching careers, most women differ from their male colleagues in interests, aspirations, expectations, educational backgrounds, and life experiences. Few are able to adapt to the masculine domain. I began to see why my mostly male department didn't like my doctoral program.

The deeper I went into the data, the more I began to realize that statistically I was a loser, destined to follow countless other women out the back door of higher education. My personal life differed from the lives of the majority of university women faculty, 51 percent of whom are not married, and 67 percent of whom have no children. My husband, however, fit the male profile perfectly. Eighty-nine percent of men in the universities are married, and 57 percent have two or more children.

And the personal lives of academic women differ not only from those of their male colleagues but from other women's as well. They are far more likely to sacrifice family lives for their careers, while academic men are not. But many questions occur which the data do not answer. It would be interesting, for example, to know the statistical breakdown on marriage and children for women and men in each academic rank. (Put another way: how many female professors as compared to female instructors have husbands and children?) Are academic women different from "normal" women, and does their lack of interest in home and family therefore lead them to academic careers? Or does the male-dominated world of academe tend to drive out all but the exceptional woman, who either rejects home and family or has the stamina to cope with double responsibilities? Either way, the universities are apparently inhospitable to the woman who desires what most people consider a normal personal life.

My research led me further: I discovered that academic men and women in the universities also differ significantly in their professional qualifications. Here I am closer to the profile of the typical faculty woman who, were she working at WIU, would be worrying about her future. University women are much less likely than men to hold the PhD. Nationally, only 25 percent of women faculty in the universities have doctorates, compared with 57 percent of the men. In 1970, women earned only 13.3 percent of the doctoral degrees awarded, but 39.7 percent of the master's degrees. Although the graduate schools generally accept the same proportion of women applicants as men, and although women proportionally receive as much financial aid as men, their attrition rate is much higher than men's. In fact, the single characteristic most highly correlated with "success" —or conversely with attrition—in graduate school is sex. Men have a two and one-half times greater probability of acquiring a PhD than women. Joseph Mooney's study of Woodrow Wilson fellows—men and women selected because of their high achievement and promise—revealed that six to eight years after the women fellows entered graduate school only 16 percent had earned their doctorates, whereas 41 percent of the men had obtained theirs. However, 60 percent of the women had earned their master's degrees, which Mooney feels is probably a terminal degree for the majority of them. Why did the women fail to finish? Mooney finds one explanation in the women's inability to remain in graduate school long enough to complete their doctoral requirements. But the academic disciplines they favor explain the failure even further. Fifty-two percent of the female fellows worked in the humanities, compared with 34 percent of the males, and students in these fields traditionally take longer to acquire the PhD. In fact, female scientists were two and one-half times more likely to acquire the PhD than female humanists. Other considerations—difficult to measure statistically but no doubt important—are the paucity of women teachers of doctoral students and the masculine orientation of graduate schools. (Mooney reported his findings in the *Journal of Human Resources*, III, 1, Winter 1968.)

Women who do manage to obtain doctorates take longer to complete their degrees than men and are older when they receive them (30 percent of the women but only 10 percent of the men are past 40). Women tend to have more interruptions in their graduate school attendance, though total time in school for males and females is the same.

The facts began to make sense. Because most women are unwilling or unable to make the personal sacrifices an academic career has traditionally demanded of them, and because most academic women for various reasons settle for a master's degree or take a long time to acquire their doctorates, we find only a few women in the universities—and most of these are stuck at the bottom of the academic hierarchy.

WIU's pattern is typical. Women comprise 47 percent of the undergraduates, 31 percent of the graduate students, 45 percent of the instructors, 19 percent of the assistant professors, 10 percent of the associate professors, 9 percent of the professors, and 7 percent of department chairpersons. None of the deans and less than 1 percent of the administration are women.

Given the patterns of women in academe and a shrinking college job market, faculty women are likely to become another vanishing species. For, like me, the untenured woman is less likely to hold a doctorate than is the untenured man. So long as masculine values continue to dominate both the reward system and the probationary timetables of higher education, few women will be able to enter on a permanent basis; the masculine criteria dominating the tenure system—academic credentials, the "right sort" of publications, status, prestige—continue to select women out.

But is this situation discriminatory? Traditionally, discrimination has been regarded as an overt, individual action which fails to apply the same objective, relevant standards to all. Such policies—nepotism rules are a good example—have largely been eliminated from higher education. But research has shown that the term "discrimination" has several dimensions. Discrimination can be implicit rather than explicit, inadvertent rather than overt, and institutional rather than individual if policies, however objectively applied, nevertheless produce differential *results*. Overly stringent hiring qualifications, recruitment among sources removed from minorities and/or women, use of irrelevant aptitude or skill tests for promotion—such devices, applied equally to all, may also have the *effect* of excluding minorities or women, resulting in a largely white, male work force. Such policies can be called discriminatory.

This second definition of discrimination obviously underlies *Higher Education Guidelines for Executive Order 11246*, the affirmative action guidelines that call for universities to eliminate "any standards or criteria which have had the effect of excluding women and minorities." The *Guidelines* make it clear that universities need not employ or promote the unqualified, but they must "establish in reasonable detail" and make available the "standards and procedures which govern all employment practices," including criteria for appointment, retention, and promotion. The universities must determine "whether such standards and criteria are valid predictors of job performance, including whether they are relevant to the duties of the particular position in question." Of course the *Guidelines* acknowledge "range of permissible discretion" associated with "employment judgments," but "where such discretion appears to have operated to deny equality of opportunity...its discriminatory effects" must be eliminated.

But for universities such as WIU, the doctorate is a criterion which has "had the effect of excluding women and minorities." When WIU insists that its faculty members obtain the doctorate and teach upper division courses or lose their positions, it sets up a standard that discriminates against women, who for complex historical and cultural reasons have not acquired the doctorate in significant numbers. Such women are lost to students as teachers and as role models. Students of both sexes then perceive women as incapable, and the *status quo ante* is perpetuated. Yet no university like WIU can honestly claim that possession of the doctorate is either relevant to the duties of teaching undergraduates or a valid predictor of job performance unless it admits that 45 percent of its faculty is not qualified to teach at the college level; this is the proportion at WIU who have been retained, given merit raises, and even promoted without the doctorate. The figure is similar at many other schools.

Like other universities of its type, WIU must face this problem immediately, for my situation is not unique. Sixty percent of its women faculty and 75 percent of those without tenure do not hold doctorates. How many of these women will complete their doctorates in fields satisfactory to the male hierarchy in time to obtain tenure is anybody's guess. Unless WIU changes its policies, many will be terminated when their probationary time is up. And, given the competition for academic jobs, the probability that all their positions will be filled by women is slight, so that the percentage of women faculty is likely to decline. But even if they finish their doctorates, many of these women will also have to overcome other strongly held prejudices. These include the notions that a good university cannot hire and/or tenure faculty wives or its own graduates and that it cannot allow persons who began their teaching careers as faculty assistants, instructors, or part-time or temporary faculty to advance up the hierarchy. The cry is always for "new blood"—a revealing and appropriate image for a masculine system.

Clearly, allowing women permanent places in the ivory tower will require revolutionary changes in higher education, and such a process will necessarily begin with a re-examination of the values on which its structure is based. But this may not be as painful as it appears. For WIU, it will mean that the administration must be honest about its requirements for promotion and tenure and bring its criteria into line with its own Board of Governors' policy and that of the AAUP. The former requires 30 hours past the master's for tenure; the latter states that a university unable to recruit enough doctors to fill all its full-time teaching positions should not deny tenure to full-time teachers lacking doctorates.

Ending discriminatory policies need not affect WIU's attempt to upgrade the quality of its teaching. If an all-doctoral faculty is desirable, rewards can encourage the completion of degrees—rewards such as bonuses, lighter teaching loads, upper division and graduate courses, and eligibility for special programs. And the word "quality," like the word "qualified," should be defined broadly to include not only the traditional masculine values of credentials and publications, but also effective teaching, and the ability to establish an atmosphere of mutual support, trust, help, and cooperation. WIU's diverse student body—a lively mixture from Chicago suburbs and ghettos, medium-sized towns, small villages, and farms—should be guided by a diverse faculty, including a substantial number of women, young and old, with children as well as without, of all colors and from all social classes and backgrounds.

From the beginning, the women's movement has aimed at providing liberation for all people, not just women. If the movement succeeds in humanizing the universities, in replacing the drive for prestige with a drive to help others, men will benefit at least as much as women, and the achievement will be momentous indeed.

The Search for Talented Women

By Elizabeth Tidball

Women achievers: Who are they? What sort of educational background do they have? What is the relationship between marriage and career success? I recently gained some new insights into this group of women who, though their numbers are small, represent a valuable national resource. We hear that such women are hard to find. Why is this so? If we seriously want more talented women, what are some of the conditions we must emphasize or create in order to produce them?

Starting with a group of women who had successful careers, I examined data about their personal and educational histories in a search for patterns and possible clues to their success. In this sense my study was impersonal: it did not attempt to explore the sacrifices and obstacles, the deprivations or psychological costs, that these women faced on their road to achievement. Rather it dealt with the records of persons and the colleges that influenced them during a critical time in their lives.

Achievement for these studies was defined on the basis of inclusion in *Who's Who of American Women*, 1966-71. A 2 percent sample of all women achievers who are college graduates was randomly selected.

Information about the women was acquired from their biographical sketches; institutional information was obtained for the colleges from which they graduated for the years during which they were students from the *Biennial Survey of Education* or *Earned Degrees Conferred*. A college's record for turning out women who were achievers was calculated by relating the number of achievers (determined from the 2 percent sample) from a given college at a given time to the total number of women graduating from that college at the same time. The probabilities of being cited for achievement for graduates of women's and coeducational colleges were then correlated with selected marital and institutional characteristics. Public, private, and church-affiliated colleges of various sizes, selectiveness, and wealth were represented among the 58 women's colleges and 289 coeducational institutions from which the achievers graduated during the five-decade period from 1910-1960. Before 1920, 72 percent of women graduates emerged from coeducational colleges; in the 1950s, 88 percent. Today the figure is approximately 92 percent.

The first tabulations of these data revealed that for the five-decade period, graduates of women's colleges were more than twice as likely to have been cited for career achievement as were women graduates of coeducational colleges. All unmarried graduates were seven times more likely to be cited than those who were married. Further, if we extend these data, we conclude that of more than 4 3/4 million married women who have graduated from college during the past 60 years, 30,000 have been cited for achievement; while of the 1/4 million unmarried women who graduated during the same period, 20,000 have been recognized. From these data it can be seen that successful career women often choose life styles that differ from those of most women in our society. The relative paucity of successful married women reflects what our society expects and encourages.

The college may be an important factor in whether the talented women who enter emerge and follow the road to success. Both the married and unmarried graduates of women's colleges were more likely to become successful career women than were their coed counterparts. Thus college choice is important in whether there are more or less successful women in our society, even though it is unlikely that a girl selects a college on the basis of its reputation for graduating successful career women. Rather, at the college-going age, most girls are encouraged by parents and friends to choose a school with many social activities. This is quite different from what happens to a boy. Whether or not he marries, he is expected to have a career; so he is more likely to choose a college whose graduates have the sort of success he is seeking. But a girl, whether or not she has a career, is expected to marry. Her college choice, often made for the wrong reason or for no positive reason, is perhaps even more critical when it comes to achievement, even though marriage may help or hinder the development of her talent.

If our society is concerned with the developing of women achievers, then there must be at least two responses to these findings: (1) parents, high school counselors, and students must be made aware of the influence of the college environment on women students and encourage girls to select colleges which are concerned with developing women's best talents; and (2) society and the educational establishment must eliminate the stigma attached to unmarried women and enhance opportunities for talented married women. This change in attitudes and policies could foster freedom of college choice for women, the willingness to explore and develop personal talents, and the ability to make sound marital decisions.

A closer look at the personal data of the women achievers in the study reveals that these women share many characteristics. Regardless of the type of college from which they graduated, the proportion of achievers who were married was the same (57 percent) as were the average number of years between receiving the bachelor's degree and marriage (7), the divorce rate (6 percent), the proportion who have engaged in postbaccalaureate studies (80 percent), and the proportion who have earned doctorates (40 percent). This leads to the conclusion that an achiever is an achiever is an achiever. But the fact that married graduates of women's colleges are almost three times as likely to become successful in careers as married women graduates of coeducational colleges strongly suggests that, rather than two kinds of women, there are two kinds of educational environments: one which encourages potential achievers, and one which is startlingly inefficient in doing this. It must be concluded that coeducational colleges have been preoccupied with the needs of their men students and have virtually ignored those of women.

What, then, are some of the factors of the educational environment that can maximize the potential of women students and account for the different numbers of women achievers who graduate from women's and coed colleges? The most striking factor relates to the composition, by sex, of the faculty and student body. Simply stated, the greater the women-faculty/women-student ratio, the greater the number of women graduates who subsequently achieve. While the average number of women-achievers/women-faculty was the same in both groups of colleges (women's and coeducational), the women-faculty/

women-student ratio in the women's colleges was twice as large as that in the coeducational schools. The correlation between the number of women faculty and number of career achievers was highly significant for each decade as well as for the 50-year period during which the women achievers were students. Women teachers as role models for women students are thus a critical ingredient of a college environment that turns out talented women. In addition to serving as role models, women professors have also been found to be more concerned with the emotional development of their students and with helping them attain a deeper level of self-understanding than are male professors (A.E. Bayer, American Council on Education). This kind of development may be especially critical for talented young women in their struggle to understand themselves not only as women but also as persons, so women teachers are doubly important to them.

The relationship between men students and women achievers is just the opposite: the greater the number of men students, the fewer the number of women graduates who become achievers. This negative effect permeates the whole college environment: in the classroom, in student and student/faculty relationships, and in extracurricular activities. It is in this sense that the coeducational colleges provide a setting most like that of the wider society, a setting in which males predominate at all levels in the important activities. That men students would find a coeducational college not only affirming of their formal goals but also attractive for their psychosexual needs should be self-evident and understandable. That women students have opted in large numbers for this definition of a "natural" environment attests to their role confusion at this time of life. That educators have not recognized the distinctive requirements of college men and women is consistent with the fact that virtually all educators in policy-making positions are men whose own role models are men and who identify primarily with the young men who will be their heirs.

Other institutional characteristics were also investigated. When colleges were matched for selectivity and for faculty compensation per full-time student equivalent ("academic expenses"), neither of these variables separately or together could account for the differences in achiever output between the women's and coeducational colleges, although greater selectivity and expense were each associated with higher achiever production within each school type. Graduates of both highly selective and less selective women's colleges were at least twice as likely to become achievers as were women graduates of coeducational colleges of comparable selectivities, while for 30 percent less academic expense the less selective women's colleges graduated as many achievers as did the most selective coeducational colleges.

The relationship between college size and achiever production revealed not only an ideal size for achiever output (200-600 graduates per year), but also that this ideal is the same for both women's and coeducational colleges. Women's colleges still graduated approximately twice as many achievers as coeducational colleges wherever comparisons could be made on the basis of comparable size, while very small colleges (less than 100 graduates per year) were found to do considerably better at achiever proportion than the larger colleges (more than 1,600 graduates per year).

Other measures of women's achievement are currently under investigation, including attainment of the doctorate (1920-1972) and acceptance into American medical schools (1973). Preliminary calculations indicate that graduates of women's colleges are also more likely to achieve in these realms than are women graduates of coeducational colleges. Thus with different measures of achievement, or different eras, including the most recent, the initial findings on achiever output from the two types of colleges are reaffirmed.

The cost, in dollars, of providing an educational environment that will develop talent in women students is less than amounts spent by coeducational colleges on their men students. Nonetheless, because virtually all the women's colleges are privately financed and because they have been assumed to be places where marriageable males are hard to find, they are in grave economic difficulty. Further, at this juncture in our history, the cost of improving the environment for women in the coeducational colleges is so great that many years may elapse before the situation is even moderately rectified.

While the positive recognition of the women's colleges by the Carnegie Commission on Higher Education reinforces the points that these colleges contribute to American higher education not only by providing an important option for the education of women but also because of their unusual record in developing women who achieve, the women's colleges still need considerable moral and financial support in order to survive. Simultaneously, coeducational colleges have a responsibility to create educational environments that will facilitate the development of talent in women students.

The talented women have been found. They come predominantly from the smaller colleges rich in adult women role models who care about their students' present and future. Compared to the population as a whole, an unusually large proportion of these women are unmarried, demonstrating an either/or choice between marriage and career that society imposes; those who are married have proven that the prophets who predicted a high divorce rate for successful career women were wrong.

These are statistical findings. They are a record of the outstanding achievements of real women, of the elements of undergraduate colleges which encourage or discourage women's talents, of the biases and values of our society as they are reflected not only in the policies and programs of colleges but also in the options available to talented women. It is time for us to utilize our capabilities as educators and intelligent people to lead the way toward a more humane society in which all talent is actively encouraged and acknowledged.

Black, Female—and Qualified

By *Ruth Fischer*

"I'm not so naive that I'm not aware of two of the reasons why I got this job," says Mary Berry, who was named a provost at the University of Maryland in College Park in May 1974. "It was considered appropriate—the kind of thing a university wants to do these days and a projection of what a university wants to be." Obviously comfortable with the appointment that placed her among the highest ranking black women academics on a major campus in this country, Ms. Berry adds: "But I also happen to be qualified."

It's hardly a secret that a double-minority academic is a hot item in today's marketplace. Given the exigencies of affirmative action, many colleges and universities understandably jump at the opportunity to appoint a black woman, thus killing two birds with one carefully aimed stone. If the appointee also is highly qualified, the lucky institution can include a third bird in its one-shot prize.

Ms. Berry's credentials dispel any notion that her appointment might have been an exercise in expediency: BA and MA from Howard University, PhD from the University of Michigan, JD from the University of Michigan Law School. Fellowships from the law school and from the Civil War Round Table. Specialization in American constitutional history, American legal history, Afro-American history. Teaching appointments at five universities. Two books and a dozen articles and reviews. Membership in the Bar of the District of Columbia. Consulting jobs with the Department of Housing and Urban Development and the Department of Health, Education, and Welfare. Work for the Afro-American Bicentennial Corporation.

After completing her doctoral work and before entering law school, Ms. Berry wanted a first-hand look at the war in Vietnam. That was in 1967, when peace wasn't entirely respectable. (She is no stranger to unpopular causes.) To comply with Defense Department restrictions on civilian travel in war areas, Ms. Berry became an instant journalist. "I spent most of my time in Vietnam out in the field with a marine battalion. We travelled from the DMZ to the Delta," she reports. "When I got back to the U.S. I wrote pieces saying that we weren't winning the war. I spoke before groups like Rotary Clubs and chambers of commerce, and they'd ask: 'How can you say such things about our great war effort?'"

Her political sophistication and her scholarly achievements are impressive by any standards. Projected against her background—Southern and Depression—they strain the imagination. "My parents didn't want their children to settle for survival," Ms. Berry recalls. "They assumed that all three of us—not only their sons—would somehow go to college. And we did."

Mary Berry worked 40 hours a week in a variety of jobs through all of her undergraduate and graduate years. Next to the encouragement from her family, the most supportive influence in her life was "an inspiring high school teacher, a black woman historian, who took me under her wing. We're still friends today." Out of her experience, Ms. Berry recognizes the importance of role models for students—black, women, or both.

She frequently is asked which minority classification has the greater impact. "It's an unfair question," she observes, "because no matter how I answer it, it may prove offensive to blacks or to women. But I have found that in a professional context, being a woman is the first consideration. In a social context, being black makes a greater difference. Until the women's movement became vocal it never occurred to me that I was discriminated against as a woman. But since I've always been black, that has occurred to me all my life."

The women's movement was not particularly vocal when Mary Berry was a young student applying for admission to graduate school. The faculty male who interviewed her recited the standard litany: Are you sure you want to be a graduate student here?... We don't have many women in this program.... Women students are not usually serious about their work.... Maybe you ought to think about it for a few days to make sure you're serious and committed before you take this step.... "He probably hoped I wouldn't come back," Ms. Berry says.

While qualified women have fewer problems today, vestiges of sexism remain on all levels of the academic ladder. Some time ago Ms. Berry was being considered for a college presidency. The person who interviewed her—the only woman on the board of regents—was troubled by the fact that Ms. Berry is unmarried. "What bothers me," the interviewer said, "is that if we hire a married man we'll get two for the price of one." Ms. Berry replied: "If a wife is required maybe I'd better go out and get one." It wasn't necessary for her to point out that husbands usually don't lend themselves to full-time volunteer activity.

Confused attitudes toward women professionals are compounded if the woman is unmarried. There's a tendency, Ms. Berry has found, to expect unmarried women professionals to devote 24 hours a day to their jobs. "But the fact that I'm unmarried doesn't mean I don't have personal relationships—which may be as time-consuming and problematic as marriage. Sometimes it's as difficult to keep from marrying as it is to be married. It takes a lot of psychic energy." Ms. Berry has no set attitudes toward marriage. "For some women it's supportive; for others it's constricting. Each of us must choose whatever arrangement provides the most living space—in the psychological sense."

Her relaxed approach to alternative lifestyles characterizes Mary Berry's easy identification with the feminist movement on campus. She is a member of the Women's Caucus, comprised of faculty, graduate students, and a few undergraduates. (Most members are women; there is a sprinkling of liberal faculty males.) The Women's Caucus has been active in support of Margaret Cussler, an associate professor of sociology who filed a sex-discrimination suit in Federal District Court. Ms. Cussler, who is approaching retirement, contends that she should have been promoted years ago to the rank of full professor.

Her complaint went through two faculty committees. Mary Berry served on the first, which was asked to decide whether Ms. Cussler was a victim of salary discrimination and ruled in her favor. It recommended that she be given a raise to bring her salary in line with that of the lowest-paid male full professor. The second committee concurred on the salary question; it also concluded that Ms. Cussler had been discriminated against on the question of promotion.

"But academic tradition holds that one is promoted only when his or her faculty colleagues recommend promotion," Mary Berry observes. "So here we have a situation where appeals committee recommendations cannot be carried out, in part because of male faculty control. This case and others like it are significant because if Ms. Cussler wins, it would establish that a college or university cannot use academic tradition as a reason for not taking affirmative action."

The Cussler case, which is still unresolved in the courts, underscores Ms. Berry's belief that faculty are mistaken when they focus on the college administration as their enemy. "What they don't seem to understand is that male colleagues in their departments are the real enemy. Peer judgment makes good sense only where those who make decisions have no sex or race biases." Ms. Berry also believes that "an administrator is foolish if he or she doesn't maintain a foot in his or her discipline." She is still a tenured faculty member in the history department.

Women students who believe they have been discriminated against gravitate to Mary Berry's office. She usually refers them to the Human Relations Program Office. One student complained that male professors who schedule exams at night do so in disregard of women's problems. (There have been several cases of rape on the campus.) Another student complained that the textbook in a course on personnel management was sexist. (The professor maintained the student had misinterpreted the book.) Another student quoted a male professor as saying: "You wouldn't want to hire a woman because they're habitually late to work and they eventually get pregnant." (The offending faculty member promised to be more careful in the future.)

While her involvement in the women's movement is strong, Mary Berry reports that her primary interest "is still the race question"—on faculty and student levels. She knows that blacks have by no means reached a millennium in college hiring. "There's a tendency to seek out the respectable Negro who can be trusted not to be militant and not to commit damage to existing institutions. The colleges want 'someone who fits in well, the kind of person you'd like to take to the faculty club for a drink, someone just like the rest of us.' And once they discover such a Negro, they're inclined to say, 'We've made our contribution to affirmative action and to democracy,' and stop at that."

In another manifestation of tokenism, minority academics are frequently overused, Ms. Berry reports. "Most of us are swamped with requests to serve on boards and committees. And one day we wake up and find we're listed by organizations we know nothing about. This happens to black women, to women with Spanish surnames, to Indian women, to Chicana women. It's as though someone out there were saying: Indians... Indians... we need a woman who's an Indian. Or: we need a woman with a Spanish surname. Or a black."

Ms. Berry hopes her presence on the 33,000-student campus will help to increase black enrollment, which now stands at 6 percent. (Nationally, blacks comprise 8.3 percent of all students in degree-granting institutions, according to Census Bureau figures.) College Park admissions officers hope that within the next few years they can raise their black student ratio at least to the level of black high school graduates in Maryland, which now stands at 15.7 percent.

Considering College Park's proximity to two major cities with large black populations, that should not be difficult. The flagship campus of the state university system is six miles from Washington and 30 miles from Baltimore. But an aura of Southern gentility persists on the Mason-Dixon-line campus that dates back to 1859, and this may dim its appeal for any except the tradition-bound. Except for the sleek new School of Architecture, all 228 buildings on the 1,300-acre, rolling campus are primly neo-Georgian and monotonously red-brick. At regular intervals a carillon chimes "Maryland, My Maryland"—and the underrepresented black student might look around and ask: *Whose* Maryland?

It's a tough question. Southern gentility and neo-Georgian architecture notwithstanding, a black woman who is a chief academic administrative officer may come up with some new answers. Mary Berry recalls the widespread publicity at the time of her appointment, and says: "It changes the image that this is a big, white university—that everyone here in a position of power and influence is white."

Jacquelyn Mattfeld of Brown

By Nina McCain

When Jacquelyn Anderson Mattfeld finished her doctoral work at Yale in the early 1950s, after being fired as a research assistant because she became pregnant, she couldn't get a teaching job. She had several strikes against her. She was a woman, with two small children. She had a husband in the same field, music history. And she had no teaching experience on the college level...because Yale had no female teaching assistants.

Jacquelyn Mattfeld is now associate provost and dean of academic affairs at Brown University — the top woman academic officer in the Ivy League. In 1972, she turned down an offer to be president of Swarthmore.

The dramatic change in Mattfeld's career fortunes is the result of two separate but not independent series of events — the emergence of an extraordinarily able and talented administrator and the slow, painful, often grudging, still incomplete acceptance of women in high-prestige academic circles.

In her own career, Mattfeld reveals a kind of encapsulated current history of women in higher education. Discussing her style, which she says is less "militant" than that of some of her younger women colleagues, she says:

"Don't forget, I'm 47. I've been tempered in a far different fire than women who have come in in the last few years riding the crest of the wave of HEW rulings....I've done all the dirty work. I've been the butt of all the things that used to happen to women. That doesn't mean I'm a martyr. I'm not. I'm here because I'm good. But I'm also here because people have been good to me and I don't forget it."

Like all women in top administrative positions, Mattfeld has a difficult dual role to play—she has to do her own job (in this case, several jobs) well and she has to be, as President Donald F. Hornig put it in announcing her appointment, "the conscience of the university in matters involving women."

Mattfeld does not seem to resent the double burden that charge lays on her. Throughout her career, she has been attempting to open the door wider for women and then give them an extra little shove to get through it. "If you're a woman in administration, you're concerned with and sensitive to the problems of women," she says. "It's impossible not to be. It doesn't matter if it's in your contract or not, you do it." When Mattfeld talks about the younger women on her staff, about their developing capacities and the careers she sees opening for them, it is obvious that this part of her job is not so much a duty and a responsibility as a joy and a delight.

But Jackie Mattfeld made it clear when she was discussing the Brown post and she has made it clear ever since that she is no token woman—no window dressing for an all-male administration concerned about its image. "I want to be remembered not as the first lady of the Ivy League but as a reformer," she says. "I want to expand the university, to open it up to all ages, races, sexes. I care passionately about that."

This concern for pushing back the boundaries of

the university to include groups that have been excluded grows out of her own life and experience and has been a continuing preoccupation throughout her career.

Trained as a pianist, Mattfeld received a diploma from the Peabody Conservatory of Music in 1947, a bachelor's degree from Goucher College in 1948, then studied music history at Yale, raised two daughters and taught piano privately for almost ten years before she met Mary Bunting, then president of Radcliffe, who lured her into academic administration. There followed a series of jobs with increasing responsibilities: director of financial aid at Radcliffe, associate dean of student affairs at MIT, dean of the college and then provost and dean of the faculty at Sarah Lawrence College and finally the appointment at Brown in July 1971.

In 1969 Brown had gone through probably the most highly publicized curriculum reform in the entire country. It had thrown out all the old freshman survey courses and instituted new "modes of thought" courses, opened up independent study opportunities for upperclassmen and allowed students to choose either letter grades or a satisfactory/no-credit option. When Mattfeld arrived, Brown was in the process of trying to figure out exactly what it had done in the burst of reforming enthusiasm and what it was going to do for an encore. This whole squirming package of reform and revision, plus the added ingredient of the new financial recession, was placed on Mattfeld's desk. She is responsible for the development and evaluation of curriculum, is the primary administration contact with the faculty and supervises the dean's office concerned with the academic counseling of undergraduates.

In a series of reports evaluating the impact of the new curriculum, Mattfeld has demonstrated two of her great strengths as an administrator—she researches carefully and marshals all the available information, and she gets to the heart of the matter in a straightforward, no-nonsense manner.

In her first report, issued only six months after she got to Brown, she zeroed in on the glaring weaknesses of the reform. She pointed out that if carried out as intended, the reforms would consume prodigious amounts of faculty time, and that the reformers had blithely assumed "a mass Damascan conversion" on the part of faculty—a willingness to spend more time and energy with undergraduates as opposed to graduate students and research—that simply was not realistic.

The second problem Mattfeld noted was that the new curriculum "is also a significantly more expensive style of education than the one it is expected to replace." Financial realities mean that Brown, like many other schools, will have to learn to live over the next few years with the same size, or perhaps even smaller, faculty and may have to increase enrollment from the current 4,500 undergraduates and 1,350 graduate students. In this report and subsequent ones, Mattfeld made it clear that she is in basic sympathy with the direction of the reforms at Brown, but she has urged a clear-eyed appraisal of what is and is not possible.

Faculty and students, she said, will have to "wrestle with our prejudices about liberal and professional education"; they will need to "design experiments, keep records, compare findings, discard and innovate, all within the budgetary confines."

In the course of this rigorous examination, Mattfeld said, "It is hard to imagine that we shall not all have to give up some or many of our most cherished ideas. But we shall be alive."

It is more than a little ironic that Mattfeld, who sees herself first and foremost as an educational reformer, has become the person chiefly responsible for guiding a reform-minded university through an inevitably painful reappraisal of its vaunted reforms. But Mattfeld is by no means intimidated by the task. She believes that the university "had an enormous rejuvenation of a sense of community out of the process of reform" and that some of the innovation will survive. By the same token, she is totally unwilling to let her own vision of a more open university fall victim to the budget cuts. She has recently proposed that Brown establish an Office for Resumed and Continuing Education to bring back older men and women who want to start new careers or change old ones. Following her own advice, she is asking for a modest beginning program with a very tight budget—$30,000 for the first year.

Mattfeld is convinced that unless Brown and other prestigious private institutions find ways to broaden their scope beyond the affluent and academically talented young people who are their traditional constituents, they will become "vestigial organs....We will go back to the 1930s when rich people who wanted their children enclaved sent them to these schools."

It was precisely this conviction about serving a broader constituency that led Mattfeld to reject the Swarthmore presidency in 1972—an offer that, as she explained in a letter to a member of the college's board, she was "within a hair" of accepting.

She decided against it, she explained, for two reasons. The first was that she felt she would be "too comfortable" at Swarthmore, a small liberal-arts college that represented "a world I already know and love....I am afraid I would no longer grow and develop and stay a part of our times in a habitat so genial," she wrote. The second reason, she continued, "has to do with the agonies of formal education in an egalitarian society caught in a social revolution.... The real test for education is going to be, and is already, how to provide true education—high academic standards, intellectual tools, moral judgments and values, human compassion and service—in places where it is harder to prevent hierarchy and status-seeking from choking cooperation and good relationships, where there are not enough faculty for the number of students, where research, not teaching, is the game, where the curriculum has never been man-centered, where it is harder to spot and attack prejudice of all kinds." If she was "to be of any social usefulness to those who want learning," Mattfeld concluded, she had better stay in a place like Brown rather than return to the warm and congenial atmosphere of a place like Swarthmore.

Cited by someone else, those reasons might smack of a taste for martyrdom or even of posing—pious phrases about social responsibility covering up ambition or a desire for more power. But to Mattfeld's friends and colleagues they are simply an expression of the woman. "She comes out of an earlier tradition of service in the professions," one of her assistant deans says. "She genuinely wants to be of service."

This conviction about service is both her shining strength and her greatest vulnerability. Mattfeld is the despair of friends who try to protect her. She feels that if she can be useful she should be, and that means not only handling the backbreaking load of administrative chores that come with her job and writing the endless reports which she will not do in a slipshod manner but also refusing to draw about herself that mantle of distance and aloofness which protects so many university administrators from the real human beings who are their students and faculty.

While she has had to cut down on her contacts with students, she has not cut them out altogether. Her talent for listening, her honesty and lack of pretension and her genuine concern draw people of all ages to her like a magnet. "She is peopled to death all day long," one friend says. "She is the person in the administration they feel they can turn to, who really hears them."

Mattfeld does not regard all this as an annoying distraction from the main enterprise of education. "People need other, more experienced people at points in their lives to hear them, help them evaluate, guide them. If the faculty abdicates this function, it will have to be taken up elsewhere. If the university won't increase student support services, other institutions will have to be formed to play that role."

She does not say so, but Jackie Mattfeld leaves the clear impression that she will use all of her formidable abilities to make sure the university she helps to run will not get out of the people business.

Women at Bryn Mawr

By Catharine R. Stimpson

In the fall of 1954, I was a middle-class provincial from the West who had "gone East" to college. One evening I stood near the steps of a gray stone building with a clock tower and listened to a group of young women in class blazers or black academic gowns chanting:

Ανασσα κατακαλῶ καλή
ἰὰ ἰὰ ἰὰ νίκη
Bryn Mawr, Bryn Mawr, Bryn Mawr!

Then they raised their fists and shouted, "Yea."

School cheers were old stuff to me. Had I not sat on wooden bleachers, in squalid fields or stuffy gyms, and shouted:

Two, four, six, eight,
Who do we appreciate?
Red Raiders, Red Raiders, Red Raiders.

But those cries had been in brutal English, not angular and sonorous Greek; in praise of young machismo athletes, not classical goddesses of victory. Cheers in Bellingham, Washington, had been a way of unifying a loose society—not proof, if proof were needed, of a cohesive culture. Though homesick and bewildered, I wanted to join the culture the Bryn Mawr cheers celebrated.

Four years later I graduated and periodically, at long intervals, returned. Then I was asked to write a profile. "A tired genre," I said, "the alumna going back. But not without possibility."

In a period in which colleges are more apt to think of the arts of survival than the liberal arts, Bryn Mawr has troubles. Some are local infections, others endemic to higher education.

- It has a reputation for being snobbish and self-congratulatory. The name, taken from the Philadelphia suburb in which the college is located, a Welsh word meaning high place or hill, feeds popular opinion: the nasality of Bryn; the drawl of Mawr; the foreign flavor of it all. Joseph Wright Taylor, the Quaker who founded and endowed Bryn Mawr, wrote in his will that it was to serve "the advanced education of young women and girls of the higher and more refined classes of society." Since 1885, when it opened, the college has tended to secure a secure sense of class instead of serving as a way of attaining one.

- Some people find its standards educationally old-fashioned and psychologically grueling. Bryn Mawr prefers rigorous scholarship; an historical perspective; balanced, serious, and sound conclusions. It fears that the present may prove a prison; the rhapsodic, empty rhetoric; and the subjective, a stranglehold. All undergraduates must show a proficiency in languages or in one language and mathematics. Students are to respect the things of the mind. The climate of expectation is that students will do well, even perfectly; that they will *want* to do well, even perfectly. Some students and alumnae fear that they cannot "measure up," that they will let the college down. The skeptical, one of whom called student life at Bryn Mawr an apathetic submission to a tyrannical piano teacher, say that the idea of work at Bryn Mawr is so obsessive that it interferes with doing it.

- It is small. The Undergraduate College has 887 women, which it will carefully increase to 900; the Graduate School of Arts and Sciences has 329 women, 143 men; the Graduate School of Social Work and Social Research 125 women, 54 men. Size hampers the college, of course, less than it does the graduate schools. The "miniversity" cannot compete with huge university centers for equipment, funds, faculty, students, and, except for some departments such as classics, a compelling national reputation.
- The college is a women's college. Able high school students, in their quest for a gratifying undergraduate life, look for education first but coeducation second. And the great men's colleges are now admitting women, bleeding students from the women's colleges, which were built because men's colleges were so exclusionary. Bryn Mawr's competition—Radcliffe, Swarthmore, Wellesley—now includes Princeton and Yale.
- Bryn Mawr is a private school, and subject to financial pressures. Though splendid in comparison to a black college like Bethune-Cookman, or a newer women's college like Kirkland, its endowment per student is smaller than that of Smith, Haverford, or Swarthmore. Demand has depleted its unrestricted reserves. In three years tuition has risen $1,000 to a total of $3,000. Room and board is $1,400. Since salary raises in 1972 ($300 per person) were punier than the cost-of-living rise, the faculty has, in effect, lost ground. The loyalty of its faculty to Bryn Mawr is legendary, but American professors today find bad pay less tolerable than their predecessors, and the Bryn Mawr faculty, badly paid in comparison to the national average for comparable undergraduate colleges, is dismally paid in comparison to the national

average for graduate schools. President Harris L. Wofford, Jr., says that Bryn Mawr has "drawn on the capital of loyalty and reputation," and "skated on thin ice with salaries." The diminution of federal money has particularly hurt the School of Social Work. Bernard Ross, its dean, who has been at Bryn Mawr since 1958, notes concisely, "Our financial picture is not clear, and not good." Sixty-seven percent of the undergraduates are from public high schools. If 33 percent of their families have an income of over $30,000 a year, 42 percent have an income of under $20,000. The average income of the rest is $25,000. At college, a great majority of the undergraduates have jobs. The college discourages the heavy use of graduate students as teaching assistants.

- Finally, Bryn Mawr bears the weight of a double irony. A college that cultivates reasoned analysis, whose emblem is the owl of Athena, is unreasonably judged. A college that has nurtured proud, stubborn independence finds itself harried by external forces indifferent to its passion for excellence.

The history of Bryn Mawr is a narrative of excellence. "At Bryn Mawr," an alumna wrote pungently after her retirement, "I learned to keep my eye on the ball." The origins of the college reveal courageous wills. Bryn Mawr dared, as a women's college, to offer a doctorate under its own faculty, and the first degree it awarded, in 1888, was a PhD.

The Graduate School of Arts and Sciences, though less famous than the undergraduate college, gives the undergraduate college its intellectual distinction and identity. Professors selected for scholarly talent come to Bryn Mawr because it has a graduate and undergraduate division. (One price they pay is hard work: an average semester load is two undergraduate courses and one graduate course. They also supervise a varying number of dissertations and senior honors theses and endure the standard amount of committee work.) In this rigorous atmosphere professors expect freshmen to behave as if they were graduate students. Because the faculty/student ratio is one to eight, such expectations take on a personal force. Undergraduates, if unsystematically, mingle with graduate students: in seminars, on archaeological digs, in the library, or in the halls, where graduate students "warden" (i.e., serve as counselors or advisers). Mabel Lang, the Paul Shorey Professor of Greek and secretary of the general faculty, says that without the graduate school, Bryn Mawr would be just another small, self-conscious college, proud of "producing all-round thinking people."

Bryn Mawr alumnae and alumni reflect an education devoted to professional intellectual concerns. The college puts history and philosophy in two of the four groups of courses from which students must choose nonmajor requirements and only last year permitted a major in fine arts. The higher the degree, the happier Bryn Mawr alumnae are apt to be with their undergraduate training and the more likely to be working full time. Twenty-eight and one half percent of the ABs have master's degrees, 6.6 percent PhDs, and 3 percent MDs. Sixty-eight percent of the ABs now go on to graduate school. In a survey the college completed in 1971, the alumnae/alumni, who then numbered less than 10,000, reported 1,000 scholarly articles, texts, or translations; 186 scientific treatises; 416 selections of nonfiction; 69 works of fiction; and 69 published poets. (Bryn Mawr's tradition of poets is livelier than the figures might suggest. Both Marianne Moore and Hilda Doolittle, or H.D., were members of the class of 1909.)

Not content to be the first women's college to offer a doctoral degree, Bryn Mawr was the first graduate school to found a department in social work. In 1920 it gave its first PhD in what it then called Social Economy and Social Research. During that academic year, M. Carey Thomas, president from 1894-1922, spending part of a leave on a safari in the African desert, thought up one of the department's most interesting ventures, a summer school for women workers. She believed they should have a place where they could learn the liberal arts, the value of clear thinking, and the pleasure of things of the mind. The school, now disbanded, gave Bryn Mawr a richly undeserved reputation as a red-tinctured redoubt.

If the Graduate School of Arts and Sciences is devoted to the principles of reason, the Graduate School of Social Work is devoted to the principle of a need to act for social change. Dean Ross, a slight, humorous, shrewd man, notes that the school is too reform-minded to be "a flower of radicalism" but adds that the nature of social work is to be "people-, cause-, and change-oriented." About 30 percent of its enrollment consists of members of minorities. Devising its programs, which often reach out to the community, students and faculty tend to challenge authority.

Other Bryn Mawr experiments are now entrenched enough to receive the compliment of indifference to their daring. M. Carey Thomas insisted that students seeking admission either pass the college's entrance examinations or what was then their one equivalent—those of Harvard. The college offered science for freshmen; a survey course in English; and history, economics, and politics. (Woodrow Wilson, who scorned women intellectuals, first taught the latter there.) It stressed competitive sports for women. It hired brilliant young scholars at the start of their careers, aware they might go elsewhere later, but wanting fresh energies. Its architecture—the buildings with turrets and battlements—was the first American use of Collegiate Gothic.

The first students were aware of their position. They knew how pervasive the doubt that women could offer English, philosophy, one science, Greek, Latin, and two modern languages for a college degree. They must have felt a special obligation to prove the skeptics wrong, and to gain both learning and freedom. After graduation, many were ardently progressive in their work and politics. In 1908, a member of the class of 1889 (to which Emily Greene Balch, the first woman to win the Nobel Prize for Peace, belonged), wrote to the alumnae magazine: she assumed that a number of graduates "...have been working in reform, churches, charities, and sociological investigations, (and) must have an intelligent knowledge of Socialism...their viewpoint would be of interest."

Many Bryn Mawr ceremonies began then: the re-enactment of an English May Day, which once featured real sheep and real oxen; Lantern Night, a rite of initiation for freshmen in which Greek hymns are sung. For the most part, Bryn Mawr rituals are either symbols of communal purpose, or, like hoop-rolling, the games of bright, inventive people who respect the classics and Anglo-Saxon traditions, who are accustomed to comfort, but who abjure flash. Though less high seriousness informs the traditions now, they add up to a local calendar, a way of measuring time that exists only at Bryn Mawr.

Wise historians of Bryn Mawr have warned me not to let M. Carey Thomas carry me away. However, much about the early Bryn Mawr reflects her formidable personality and ambition. She succeeded the more genial and prudent James E. Rhoads, in part through the efforts of relatives, among them her father, on the board of trustees. (She set the precedent of installing able young women who then stay on to serve with distinction. Marion E. Park followed her in 1922, Katharine E. McBride in 1942.) Thomas was a passionate, militant feminist, who worked in the women's movement. Her biographer, whose job several of my friends and I envy, quotes an entry from a diary she kept in 1871 when she was 14:

> If I ever live and grow up my *one* aim and concentrated purpose *shall be* and *is* to show that women *can learn, can reason, can compete* with man in the grand fields of literature and science and conjecture that open before the nineteenth century, that a woman can be a woman and a *true* one without having all her time engrossed by dress and society.

She herself fought her way to a *summa cum laude* at the University of Zurich. But Bryn Mawr was her arena and her proof. She articulated a principle that Bryn Mawr still accepts: that enlightened education will eventually lead to social progress. She saw no reason, however, why the life of the mind should be frumpy. Her taste—one hears of red velvet chairs and bronze peacocks—was exotic, flamboyant, and luxurious.

Unfortunately, she had moments of philistinism, prejudice, and despotic bossiness. Student self-government came to Bryn Mawr in 1891 in rebellion against her. (A student who devised its structure later became the first woman to make a nominating speech at a national Presidential convention.) A tradition of strong faculty control over admissions, curriculum, and appointments—over who will be taught, what will be taught, and who will teach—began in 1916 for much the same reason. Against her trustees' wishes, she put teak in the entrance of the M. Carey Thomas Library started during her reign, and when she died in 1935, her ashes, as she had asked, were buried in its cloisters.

After her retirement, Bryn Mawr's commitment to scholarship remained steadfast. So did the institutional morality that was its Quaker heritage. Like most places, Bryn Mawr has been selectively blind while priding itself on its vision. Its attitude toward blacks was one of benign bigotry. It has bogs of complacency and corners for gossip. Yet the community tries to act on its principles of honor, fairness, honesty, civility, and a respect for other persons that balances kindliness and letting them alone. An editor of the college paper said that to become an outcast a student would have to slander the Quakers, cheat on exams, be a kleptomaniac, and/or "knowingly" sell bad dope—sins that either traduce Bryn Mawr's traditions or violate the rights and safety of others. A professor told me that he knows no more about his colleagues than he "needs to know, wants to know, and deserves to know."

In 1959, Bryn Mawr, like Haverford and Swarthmore, refused to take federal funds because it meant taking loyalty oaths as well. In 1968, the student newspaper reported that the FBI had investigated a black who had gone to a conference of black students. The next time the FBI saw the student, she was in the office of a trustee who was serving as her counsel. In 1970, Bryn Mawr was the only school in Pennsylvania both to denounce and decline to sign the Pennsylvania Higher Education Assistance Act. Later declared unconstitutional, it made the reporting of disruptive students mandatory if schools were to receive state aid for scholarships and loans. Today, alumnae go to corporate meetings to vote the college's stock on such issues of corporate responsibility as South Africa, war-related activities, and employment of minorities and women.

Even as Bryn Mawr kept its conscience and its head, it became less isolated and more open to the world at large. In 1928, for example, men attended a hall party, for the first time as far as I was able to discover. Though the proportion of Quakers was and has been steady at around 5 percent, the proportion of other Protestants began to fall; the proportion of Jews, for whom Bryn Mawr never had a quota, started to climb. Today, the number of Catholics, in part a response to the ecumenical spirit that has made non-Catholic schools acceptable, is growing. In spring 1973, 200 students, including a lot of the Catholics, went to a model seder. Compared to the alumnae before 1915, more and more Bryn Mawrters married, 92.7 percent of the classes between 1951 and 1955, the years in which femininity as usual was so popular. Their husbands were most commonly professors, lawyers, doctors, or executives, about 35 percent from the prestigious neighboring schools of Haverford, the University of Pennsylvania, and Princeton.

If the Bryn Mawr marriage rate was conventional, the divorce rate was below average and the accomplishments of the wives well above. So were those of its single women. For Bryn Mawr was showing what educators, social ecologists, feminists, and the colleges themselves are rediscovering: the fact that the graduates of all the women's colleges do more in the world at large, earn more doctorates, and are more apt to go into science and mathematics than the women graduates of coeducational colleges. In 1973, the Carnegie Commission on Higher Education cautiously, but surely, accepted evidence that "the larger proportion of achievers among graduates of women's colleges was related to the larger proportion of women on the faculties of those institutions. In addition, there was a high negative correlation between the ratio of men to women among undergraduates in coeducational institutions and the ratio of women achievers among their graduates." A tragedy of the women's colleges is that, like an endangered species, they had to come close to extinction before their preserve was recognized.

Bryn Mawr prides itself on the fact that its undergraduates are women. The students it carefully selects are bright. The median verbal SAT scores are now in the high 600s, the median math scores in the mid-600s. Once at Bryn Mawr, students tend to stay and the college likes to keep them. The freshman academic drop-out rate is less than 1 percent; between 75 and 80 percent of an entering class graduates. The Graduate School of Arts and Sciences has, for the most part, been sensitive to the complex patterns of the lives of postgraduate women: 60 percent of its students go to school part time.

However, society has been less willing to accept the talents of a Bryn Mawrter than Bryn Mawr has been. Of the 2,500 alumnae who said they had encountered "major obstacles in pursuing their chosen activities," 923 alumnae report having job difficulties because they are women. Of those brilliant, funny, ingenious, well-trained, hard-working, promising women who had sung in Greek on October nights to the goddess of wisdom and in Latin on May mornings to the sun—14 percent became secretaries when they took full-time, paying jobs.

Nor was the structure of the American family, in which so many Bryn Mawrters believe, flexible enough to adapt itself to their interests. Of the 2,500 alumnae who confronted those obstacles, others said the trouble "related to combining motherhood with a career." In 1971, a woman, one of the most brilliant of her time, wrote:

> How have the so-called "women's liberation" issues affected me? In my part-time profession as a writer, not at all. In my full-time profession as a wife and mother I wrestle with women's liberation dragons every day.
> The most powerful dragon of all is one of my making—my (culturally conditioned?) conviction that if I ever really let out all the stops and pursued my career as vigorously and tenaciously as I would like to, I would do irreparable damage to my children and my marriage.... Intellectually the

> years at Bryn Mawr were the freest of my life....
> My life has turned out more or less as I always expected that it would. Now maybe this is the key. Is it all predetermined by the expectations? I sincerely hope that my daughter's will be higher.

To loosen the knot of conflict between its graduates and the society into which they would graduate, Bryn Mawr no longer uses the solvent of a self-consciously political women's movement. Even today many find the new feminism irrelevant to Bryn Mawr, irritatingly preachy, unfair to motherhood, or excessively frank about sexuality. Rather, for the most part, the college has treated its students as if they were potentially more than equal to anything and anyone.

As equipment for use after graduation, the college fostered the myth of the Bryn Mawr Superwoman. Transcending historical conditions, she was omnicompetent. If people thought women were stupid or useless, Bryn Mawr or a Bryn Mawrter herself would refute them. As someone remarked to me, "We had Miss McBride out there. She was showing the world what women could do." A Bryn Mawrter neither needed nor wanted a movement. Indeed, an admission of need might prove tantamount to an admission of failure at superwomanship. In 1971, according to its "class notes," those ignored documents of social history, the alumna writing of the class of 1961 said:

> Women's lib hasn't changed the working scene... the tactics of the lib leaders border on the absurd though their aims are desirable...the lib movement has little effect on their lives, and they are not active in the movement except on the personal level by working in a field considered reserved for men.

The myth of the superwoman was congruent with the college one alumna described in this way: "After the generation of pioneers, Bryn Mawr got very smart girls from very nice families." Perhaps they shifted from women who wished to be exemplary rebels, which demanded great strength of individual character, to women who wished to be both individualistic and exemplary, but not that rebellious.

The Bryn Mawr I attended was pervasively indifferent to politics, not just to "women's rights." In retrospect, the summary of my class in the yearbook projects us as steamily precious, well-scheduled apprentices in the house of learning:

> On the whole, we have enjoyed four years of detachment; "outside events" have troubled us little. Suez, the Hungarian revolt, the reelection of Dwight Eisenhower, Sputnik, Explorer, and Recession have not touched us as deeply as tomorrow's mid-semester or the next day's paper.

Political opinions, when expressed, were conventional or even unconventionally conservative. In October 1960, an editorial in the student newspaper welcomed a Moral Re-Armament handbook because it gave students a creed with which to fight Communism and to help America scourge itself of those domestic sins that were "impediments to success in the Cold War." Some faculty sharply protested. Yet in the same year, 62 Bryn Mawr and Haverford students picketed Woolworth's in behalf of the civil rights movement. For the first time, as many students as faculty members preferred a Democrat to a Republican as president.

During the next decade or so Bryn Mawr became a gentler microcosm of other American campuses. Students officially supported the Berkeley Free Speech movement and antiwar activities. Blacks, admitted in numbers for the first time, organized. So did feminist students, who accused Bryn Mawr of betraying the legacy of M. Carey Thomas. People organized a handful of sit-ins, to demand change, and colloquia, to articulate a discontent of a bitterness and dimension not before seen at Bryn Mawr. An administrator who went to the colloquia said ruefully, "It was awfully hard to take."

Among the Bryn Mawr graduates of the sixties were several Weatherwomen, among them Diana Oughton, who was killed in the explosion in a townhouse on West 11th Street in New York that was being used as a "bomb factory." The people to whom I spoke about Bryn Mawr radicalism believed her death a grievous personal tragedy but an anomaly, for to them Bryn Mawr creates civic leaders, concerned citizens, and reformers—not revolutionaries. Yet one knows Bryn Mawr can beget or intensify the sense of privilege that, in its turn, can beget or intensify both guilt and the belief that one has a special obligation, even the promise of a special skill, to destroy privilege itself.

Since 1960, through external and internal pressure and accommodation, Bryn Mawr has irrevocably modified its ways. The "slow and stately" process, which makes some impatient and others sure that Bryn Mawr is too inert ever to alter, guarantees that the change that comes will be secure. The atmosphere is looser and easier. Parietals in halls reserved for women have been abolished. Marijuana is a commonplace. The infirmary prescribes birth control devices and gives information about abortions. Students participate on powerful faculty committees. A group is studying ways in which they may contribute to tenure decisions. Bryn Mawr offers some classes about blacks and women and six interdisciplinary majors and concentrates. The students, says Mabel Lang with poker wit, once gave "one...the feeling that undergraduates preferred their men teachers because they were more exciting, but now they have a sense of responsibility to their women professors."

The first personnel administrator, a Bryn Mawr alumna, has been at work since 1971. For some time now, the black maids and porters, "Rhiny" or "Robert" to me while I was "Miss Stimpson" to them, have not been required to live on-campus. Some have become hall managers, a job only white women once held. In 1970, a woman who worked in one hall wrote to the college newspaper to respond to an earlier letter that had complained about the maids. After criticizing white students who flattered black students but bossed black maids, she said: "As a black woman first and a college employee second, I must tell you that the days are gone when a maid had to be afraid to look squarely at a student."

As the institution was changing, so was the administration. Some alumnae complained when Harris Wofford was offered the presidency of Bryn Mawr, arguing that no man should head a women's college, let alone Bryn Mawr, until a woman was installed as head of Harvard. But if a women's college is to have a male president, it might as well be Wofford. A tall, spare, dark man, shyer than I expected, he is wry, thoughtful, idealistic, and affectionate, married to a strong, cordial woman and the father of three children. It must have been difficult to come to a proud college that had a history of women presidents of great stature. Merely to replace Katharine McBride would have been hard.

He takes seriously the obligations with which he was charged when he was asked if he would become president—to open Bryn Mawr up "somewhat more to the world, but also [to] respect and maintain its academic standards and scholarly tradition." A lawyer, he was a civil rights activist and a Peace Corps official. Among the pictures in his office are the first Bryn Mawr class and faculty; Katharine McBride and Martin Luther King, Jr., both in academic robes, talking; and John and Robert Kennedy. Some of his rhetoric—his talk of the "challenge" of keeping Bryn Mawr alive—has a faint ring of the New Frontier, but he is free from a domineering "I'm the take-charge man around here" manner. In the spring of 1971, his first year at Bryn Mawr, the student newspaper complained that he was not the master of his house. He replied, "It is not 'my house' and no one is going to become 'master' of Bryn Mawr."

The new young dean of the undergraduate college, Mary Patterson McPherson, is widely and justly respected. She came to Bryn Mawr as a graduate student in philosophy whose specialty was the British Idealists. She was, she says, "pulled into the ethos of the institution." Even students who find her reserved, or reformers who think her educational philosophy conservative, praise her judgment, wit, integrity, and devotion to the college. "Everyone in higher education is going to try to hire her away," I was told. She appears to have assumed, or to have been given, the burden of becoming, within and beyond the institution, the personification of the intelligent woman leader, and as such, she is Katharine McBride's symbolic replacement. People point out the physical resemblance between the two: both are tall and impeccably mannered; their heads might be models for a Greek statue.

The director of the Office of Career Planning and Placement is now a gentle, modest, perceptive woman, Dolores Brien, who worked for a Catholic women's organization before she decided, at 37, to get a PhD. Once she earned the degree, she decided she would like to work on behalf of women. She meets a multiplicity of needs: for more career planning and counseling; for some warning about the hostility of the world toward ambitious women; for suggestions of alternatives to graduate school for students in a college that so treasures academic success.

Students say the 1970s mood is serene and more collegiate. The college physician reports that more people are drinking, as they are on other campuses. They also worry about jobs. English is the most popular major, but in 1973 history and biology were the most popular single courses. Simultaneously, the interest in the classics has been renewed: Bryn Mawr had to offer two sections of "baby" (or elementary) Greek in fall 1973. I am unsure of the significance of it all. One student suggests people feel better because of early reforms. Some people believe it represents a turning simultaneously away from politics to self-interest and the private life and toward tradition for stabilizing the self. Others suggest that the pendulum of history is at work. A distinguished Latin professor said, "It swings every 10 years. We keep fully staffed and wait for it."

When I visited in 1973, the tenor of academic life reminded me uncomfortably of my own in the fifties. Sitting in classes, the largest of which must have had no more than 50 students, I was surprised at how little they talked except to ask questions of fact. The rooms lacked the edge of skepticism, of tentative rudeness, that often marks promising inquiry. I wondered if my alien presence was inhibiting. Then Eugene V. Schneider, the chairman of the sociology department, told me a story. He said he had handed out 3 x 5 cards in his theory class. In the first hour students were to write down any questions they might have. Only about a third put anything down. But, Schneider said, the papers they handed in later were very good.

Perhaps the conservative scholarship in which Bryn Mawr specializes necessarily requires diligence and passivity. Since the persistent clarity of Bryn Mawr's identity has come from its devotion to the principles of scholarship, to abandon them would be to abandon the nerve of Bryn Mawr. Students are asked to defer gratification, but they receive the personal attention, even if attention seems like a demand, that only a small institution can provide. Still, Bryn Mawr has more than its share of dutiful diligence. Student passivity often may be less an absorption in ideas and methods than an apathy that threatens to collapse into boredom. Binding the faculty, I sense a fear that new methods will, like a loony Samson, bring that temple of scholarship, erected with such sacrificial care, crashing down.

Bryn Mawr cannot order up institutional vitality any more than I could order up maturity when I was an undergraduate. However, it has sensible ideas that may bring in new zest. Elizabeth G. Vermey, one of the ablest members of my class and now director of admissions, is inventive about recruitment. She wants to dispel the notion that Bryn Mawr is a citadel to which few are called and fewer chosen. The canny know that Bryn Mawr must enlarge its reputation in the black community, in the Southwest, and in the West. Now 65 percent of the undergraduates are from Pennsylvania and the Northeast. Seventy percent of the alumnae live between Virginia and Maine. They need to continue what Katharine McBride did to bring students to Bryn Mawr from unlikely places. I went there, for example, because she asked me to meet her in Seattle when I was in high school. How she got my name is a mystery, for I had never written to Bryn Mawr. I think she said to me, "You seem like the kind of person we would like to have at Bryn Mawr," and I thought to myself, as my mother and I drove 90 miles home after tea, "I want to go to the school where she's the president."

The general pattern of Bryn Mawr's plans apparently follows the requests that were made of Harris Wofford. To maintain its scholarly tradition, it has undertaken to raise $21 million by 1976, $12 million of which will become a part of the endowment. The income will be spent on faculty salaries, student financial aid, and the library. Though Bryn Mawr has one of the 10 best collections of incunabula (books printed before 1501) in the country, it cannot buy the new books it needs. Wofford believes it might be fatal to Bryn Mawr if the financial support were inadequate and the quality of the faculty therefore damaged.

To raise the money, the college needs the support of friends and the approval of corporations. To justify spending money on a small university it uses the argument that the health of American higher education has always depended upon its diversity, the quality of American students upon their range of options. Successful fund raisers, of course, depend on organic links to capitalism and the American class structure. To condemn such links is as stupid as to confuse a wave and the sea. Take away the wave, the sea will still be there. Take away the private schools, capitalism will still be there—though some signs of status, some powerful old-boy networks, and some elements of consciousness and conscience would surely disappear.

To open Bryn Mawr up "somewhat more to the world," Bryn Mawr has a congeries of plans. They include:

- Building a postbaccalaureate pre-medical school program.
- Developing a four- to five-year BA/MA program, particularly for transfer students. (Wary of inbreeding, the college is apt to question undergraduates who want to go on to Bryn Mawr graduate school.)
- Increasing ties between the campus and business, including an "executive-in-residence" from

time to time.

- Continuing the 1976 Studies Program, a four-year series of seminars, lectures, and so on that relate the premises of the Declaration of Independence to the contemporary world.
- Renewing and creating international exchanges, research, and study. (A $50,000 anonymous donation was given to set up such a program with Africa. Alumnae in Japan are raising money for similar work.)

However, the world with which Bryn Mawr must now work out an arrangement is a local train stop away: Haverford. Bryn Mawr, when it began, became radically feminist in order, paradoxically, to work for sexual equality. Now, to remain a women's college, it may work with a men's college toward equality. In the process, it may try warily to offer sanctuary both to the new radical feminists who care if male professors outnumber women, as they do, and to those who find such voices distasteful.

Bryn Mawr may have done little to repair the split in my character between thought and feeling, but I also learned more by meeting standards than by violating them—even if violation had been legitimate rebellion. And I want Bryn Mawr to survive. It gave me a sense of standards, of the distinction between substance and fluff. It taught me to respect the exact and the scrupulous and to have faith in the eventual efficacy of thought. After Bryn Mawr, I was surprised to hear women say that they had never had a woman friend or that going into intellectual competition with men scared them. The college has, at its best, grace and courage. I asked Ellen Reisner, the executive director of the alumnae association, if she thought a place like Bryn Mawr could survive. "Well," she said, "if we're going down, I'm going down fighting."

Two of my recent Bryn Mawr memories are vivid.

One fall, I had gone into the bookstore. Books about women were next to books for children. "That's Bryn Mawr," I thought. "It produces feminists, but it won't ever be a feminist school." In January, I went back to find out what students bought. Art and archaeology, I was told. Faculty and alumnae books, drama, current affairs, fantasy, religion. "They buy books," the manager said, "more than people in other places do. They care about them. They have taste, humor, and wit. They're tough." Then I noticed that the books about women and the women's movement had been relocated away from the children's section. I asked why. "The old arrangement made a lot of people angry," the manager said.

The old chapel, where M. Carey Thomas used to speak, on the third floor of Taylor Hall, is now a storeroom. On one side is the public information office, on the other side the records office—all part of any modern college. But on a circular iron staircase leading to a garret, as if it had been placed there casually but preserved carefully, was a small statue of a Greek figure, handsome in itself, and a reminder of what from the past we must offer to the future.

In 1974, as of January, applications for admission were up 70 percent.

Women and War

By Kate Millett

Necessarily this concerns a journey. Travels not only to certain women's colleges which have now become places of very real personal concern to me, but, inescapably, travels into my own past as well. I went back to the South; I went home to the Middle West. So I will try to tell not only what I saw and heard, but what happened to me and what I felt.

When we started up to Vassar that Monday in May 1970, the strike had just been called. Of course, it seemed at first only an accident, a delayed response, a fluorescent bulb tuning up, taking so long it looked for a time as if it were *not* about to happen. And Cambodia itself a vast idiot blunder, like any tragedy, as lethal as it was inconceivable. But I did not leave town with this most on my mind. Initially there were things closer to my life: the trip ahead of me to the women's colleges, the women's colleges I'll visit, the issue of women's education, the chances of organizing these students—and naturally, Women's Liberation—its immediate reality, its most recent drama.

Over the weekend, at the great annual powwow, entitled with perhaps excessive irony "The Congress to Unite Women," the movement, awash in its endless factions and squabbles, had scarcely taken account of external politics. While Nixon sounded his victory, we faced the issue of lesbianism. All things considered, we faced it pretty well.

Lesbians at the Congress Friday night had insisted on recognition and acceptance. Of course, Women's Liberation had never given them either. When we first went out to picket years ago, we learned to live with catcalls convicting us of ugliness, sexual frustration, and penis envy. But at the word *dyke* we dissolved on the pavement. Magical language—sexism thrives on it—and the accusation of homosexuality kept us all in line. Lesbians had had enough. They came on camp and pleasant: guerrilla theater, signs like "Super-dyke loves you," pastel T-shirts with "Lavender Menace" stenciled on them—Betty Friedan's put-down phrase now a joke.

The lesbians were cheered, and for some who cheered them it must have been their first Women's Lib meeting. The worst rumors seemed confirmed: we *were* a lesbian plot.

Each woman on the scheduled "panel of stars," unwilling to wear that murderous label, abdicated in relief, delighted to turn the evening over to its takers. Healthy anarchy followed—four hours in which confrontation grew into dialog. There were perhaps 500 people present, and 100 must have spoken from the mike or from their chairs, as the spirit moved them. More remarkable, all were heard, and heard with respect. People were honest about their fears of homosexuality, their hangups, their panic, their prejudices. We were decent to each other that night. It looked as though the Congress might, after all, unite women.

When Ruth Gage Colby spoke later, she spoke of the war, the atrocity reports she had seen at the United Nations, the news in lights on Times Square that night declaring Nixon's all-out campaign in Cambodia. Everyone cheered her speech but no one heard it. Knowing her to be a feminist from the days of the international movement and its dedication to pacifism, and being myself an advanced case, a "pacifist freak," whose grandest ambition was to influence Women's Liberation toward militant nonviolent revolution, even to declared pacifism, I had to ask her when she thought the movement could talk of peace. She answered me, "Not yet."

The next two days of the Congress degenerated into our own war—a grand new leftist hiss-and-shout debacle, presumably fought over the issues of class and elitism. Both are vital matters. For whatever perfectly explicable sociological reasons, Women's Liberation is still, to all our regret, a white middle-class movement. But the proponents of class discussion appeared to be largely graduate students, persons affected by the male Left's habitual manner of hostility, whose style hopelessly alienated the majority. Most depressing of all, there were just not enough black women and still fewer white working-class women to really speak up and be heard as the gay folk had been—who, after all, had been real lesbians to rap with, and who, as a result, had caused us to confront and transcend our old terror in the face of homosexual baiting, finally passing a resolution in support of homosexual women.

The class confrontation, inauthentic, ended in obstruction which only further distracted our attention from a major issue. Sunday the Congress ended by repudiating itself. Everyone went home feeling rotten; I felt particularly rotten. Friday night we had seemed sisters. By Sunday we were enemies again. My own job of serving as peacemaker among factions, with its eternal requirements for patience and optimism, had exhausted me. And I had Cambodia on my mind, too. I felt dejected and humiliated that we pull hair and shriek, too inward-turned and insecure to relate to the files of Vietnamese nationals, shopkeepers and tradesmen, women and children, VC kids, lined up in schoolhouses waiting to be shot, their blood all over the cement walls like Aztec pyramids. (The Congress had been held in a school, too.) And the trucks came at 4 AM to cart off the corpses from the 2 AM slaughter. I kept hearing how it must sound in those rooms—the cries of basic terror, the pleas for life, the screaming. Asians, my Fumio's own color and kind.

I drove to Vassar the next morning with Barbara Rugen. Just before I left, friends from my own Columbia Lib called to say there would be a strike and we would join it, writing a Women's Liberation statement on the war. They knew I was off on my long-planned hegira to a bunch of women's colleges and so couldn't be at their meeting. Did I have any ideas? Since I really didn't know either how Women's Lib could relate to the war, and, like all of us, had been cowed by the draft issue into an unworthy silence based on the impression that we were unqualified to comment, I threw off the top of my head, "Think about the war and sexism," and wished them luck.

The Avis car had a hole in it, boiled over, and had a blowout on the highway. Driving up, we started to talk about the strike. It seemed the wrong time to visit these colleges. Women's Liberation is surely small potatoes to a war, a matter for the male Left to polemicize upon and everybody's peace movement to march about. I imagined I would see women's colleges at their most irrelevant moment. Nothing could have been more mistaken, no moment better to observe them than when confronted with a great national issue, their strengths and weaknesses tested against the total problem of life and death, and no more crucial test of Women's Liberation itself than to see if it could find a general humanist analysis which might explain militarism.

And so we hashed it over on the road, Barbara playing devil's advocate for the male revolutionary thesis that there must be violence, while I inquired who should be murdered, how it served the revolution to kill, to commit its own crimes, to corrupt its ideal of justice, to prepare the way for counterrevolution, and to increase the human suffering it advertised itself as committed to relieve. We came to agree — because we knew these guys. Knew the beard and gun delusion bellowing to "bring the war home" is a conscious psychic preparation for shooting bodies in New York streets on the part of males who won't go to Vietnam yet need to fancy themselves man enough to kill.

Then we began to try out some definitions. Violence is killing, torturing or beating persons. To destroy property is not violence. It is the destruction of property. And psychic violence? To burn the homes and shops of the poor is not violence, but unnecessary cruelty, but pointless. Then what should one substitute? Force. Force, but not violence. Force encompassing every means of mobilizing power, short of violence. One achieves it through numbers, creative intelligence and coordination. A revolution by an elite can only end in a police state. The thousands who loved the revolution imposing it upon the millions whose revolution it was not, and who therefore hate it, enduring it only as long as coercion succeeds. Another police state would be redundant and is likely to be even more repellant than the one we know.

What are the possibilities of a popular revolution in America? How many of us are on the outside and alienated from the Establishment? Surely students, the blacks and the poor. And women. The male Left still dreams that the hardhat and the flag-decal trucker are essential. It disregards working-class women because it can see them neither as persons nor as workers, though they are the largest group of exploited labor. Women are crucial because they are so many. And having so nearly nothing, they have nothing to lose. As we talk, we begin to conjure up a revolutionary strategy, one aware it can never win through the violence monopolized by government's vastly superior armament, but one morally committed not to use such methods anyway. Considering the system and its complexity, the vulnerability which follows from that, one could project its weakness in areas such as communications. Bell Tel and the U.S. Mail alone a nice start on a general strike, with provisions to deliver welfare checks, methods to avoid the ugliness which takes over in a society when food stops coming in.

Barrelling along the spring highway, how magnificent an educational project it seems to redirect Americans. The hope of revolutionary change, possibly giving us all the faith that nonviolence requires. Nonviolence—with Gandhi it took mysticism, but then he was dealing with men who would require that to offset their acculturated violence. To watch and praise it, yes—but not to participate. And this is no nonsense about natural gentleness or genetic loveliness, but sociological fact. Nor does that rule out the bitchiness, the temper we all have, the anger. And yet we are also a backward people, so oppressed we do not even relate to politics. But Gandhi's Indians were as well, Mao's peasants always. Could it be that our nonviolence, which we have always seen as disarmament, the defenseless condition necessary to rule us, the very epitome of our oppression—could it be an asset if widely used, a better place to start, a better grasp on a more human method of political struggle? And as we discuss how little ingenuity is actually devoted to nonviolent tactics and training, we talk about practical methods of dealing with concrete cases of assault in demonstrations and the thousand possibilities which must lie in technological sabotage.

Suddenly, we're at Vassar. Down to earth. The Libbies who meet us seem strangely depressed. At dinner we start to rap on war and sexism. How could they have a war without masculinity? How are virility and the warrior cult induced? The handful of students turn sullen and silent. They put us down. I'm accused of faulty pedagogy. "You don't know the situation here." "Fine. Tell me." I'm not told, but bit by bit we do learn it.

I've been wondering all through dinner if I'm using the right fork. Nearly sick in this heartbreakingly beautiful place—plum-tree-filled, its glamorous old buildings weighing on me with all the heaviness of the past. I suppose I've hated Vassar all my life. Growing up in the Midwest, Vassar symbolized fancy-assed ladies' schools, a particular target of our provincial class hatred because it was female. Harvard was hated with respect; Princeton with envy. Vassar was once the summit of all the schools I couldn't go to because I was poor, and lucky my mother could put me through the state university. Convent prep made a scholarship and its scores impossible. And who was there to inform me about scholarships? The old man had lit out four years before. Including the rich relations, no one gave a damn or a nickel at that point. It was my father's opinion that Kate needn't go to college anyway. Yet, finally here I am at Vassar. I have even learned to revere it as an early women's college, one of the first places where women could learn. And class be damned, that's still something. And so I sit there astonished;

the very students who, down at the Congress, when I asked them if I might come, were so friendly, so eager, so welcoming, tell me now to shut up and leave them alone. I don't know the situation, but it does begin to manifest itself.

It was once the custom at Vassar to take coffee in another room after dinner. Tonight the room is to house a student strike meeting. Changes. Through the doors one sees the coffee cups banked high. Something of the same thing. Barbara and I are not invited. Our student friends appear to attend only out of a dogged futility one might call responsibility of the most onerous sort, and they will not speak. Though its members are on strike, Vassar Women's Lib will take no stand on the war. It's then that I see the boys. They *are* the meeting. They appear also to be the strike. I had forgotten Vassar had acquired men after it refused Yale's proposal of a boa constrictor marriage which was clearly assimilation.

Barbara and I go out for a drink—an occasion to decipher the terrifying defensiveness that hit dinner. The friction hurts. We feel we are a burden. Maybe we should leave. But the put-down seemed so unreal, so tangential. We sense that it's a diversion from something still more painful. And there's a group rap on education at Vassar scheduled next, called just for my benefit. So we stay. Vassar is a conundrum now.

At the rap, I start as I always do by saying I'm writing on Women's Lib and the women's colleges and need student help and advice as to what I should say—insight into the undergraduate world they know. The discussion goes splendidly. The eight undergraduates construct a picture of alienation from classes and official learning which is not only a comment on colleges today but, more pertinently, a comment on the destructive character of the kind of education (both formal and social) which women receive. There was a consensus that male students are respected and deferred to by a faculty which condescends to all women and is even now in the process of "upgrading" itself by weeding out or paring down the number of women on its staff. Listening, one felt academic matters might be passed over lightly, so remote had such formal learning become, and so much more pressing were the thousand subtle, informal methods of teaching woman her place.

On the other side of the plush student lounge an aesthete works away at the piano. We depart for the grubby intimacy of a student's room. The rap grows warmer, more personal. Talk of classes gives way to dorm life, to weekends, to the meat market of undergraduate sexuality. And finally, some solid information on Vassar. The guys have taken over. Ninety-one of them are in charge of 1,600 Vassar women, voted into office by the girls themselves. Vassar Women's Lib is under a cloud. It has become notorious, has lost student support and credibility. It's stigmatized as lesbian. When its few members speak they may be instantly dismissed as eccentric persons representing an irrelevant point of view.

There's a strike meeting now in Noyes Hall. What if we all went and spoke at it? "Maybe you can take it over," volunteers one undergraduate in splendid fatuity, expecting Superwoman, delighted to abdicate before a miracle. The prospect is appalling. "It's your school, but we're all Women's Lib," I venture. "We'll all talk." We strike off across the grass. It seems possible—we are in great spirits until we hit the meeting. It's huge, turgid, irrelevant, bogged down in procedural nonsense about absences and incompletes for strikers. The very digressions so beloved of faculties, which I was to hear later at Barnard. We're looked at, but I cannot comprehend the looks. The great circle of house reps at the center is largely male. Men dominate the oratory, only one or two token girls contributing, talking like guys. Only one black man, urging the adoption of the Panther cause, seems to feel any emotion, but he's frustrated into self-indulgent tantrums by the others.

Our group entered the room together, but in a few moments we seem to shun each other and drift apart. We eye each other more sheepishly every moment. I'm still confident the discussion will turn, center on the reality of the war itself, offer us an opening. Time goes by, and I realize there will be no chance. I'm beginning to understand there never was one. People from several other colleges have talked, why shouldn't I? Am I letting this bunch down? It's clear they can't move. I'm from outside. I'm older. I should be less afraid. Soon I'm as impotent and speechless as at my first political meeting five years ago. We leave without a signal, utterly demoralized. I'm traumatized by my own cowardice, try to rationalize it. Of course, I'm no bigger than they, no braver, and no more invulnerable, but I had believed too that I was an organizer, full time in the movement now, with responsibility to discharge, whatever happens. And I cannot believe what has happened: a meeting so intimidating one could not speak out.

Then we're back in the dorm room assigned to us at Cushing. We have dwindled from eight to six to five. Through the final discussion we are three, and at moments two undergrads and Barbara and I. Piece by piece we come to understand "the situation" at last. The explanation is halting, obscure, and demands continual clarification and interpretation but one can resurrect from it something of what that year at Vassar had been. In December Vassar's Women's Lib had some 25 committed members, with perhaps, as is the custom, two or three times that number on the fringe. Toward the end of the fall semester, in

January, a few radical lesbians (I am using the term generically here and do not refer to any group) from New York began making pilgrimages to the campus. In February an all-women's party—with dancing—was held. The students seemed to enjoy it; then they drew back. The majority must have weighed the home in Westchester and the fellow at Yale that they were born and bred for, felt the pull of their own conflict, and fell off. Active membership went down to five.

Since then this handful has been left to carry the whole weight of the organization, producing its fliers, articles, position papers, stuff for the newspaper (still apparently controlled by women and open and sympathetic to their contributions). They had more to carry than this. They were self-acknowledged homosexuals at a women's college. Vassar has always had its quota of the latent or the discreet, who, unless discovered or informed on, might avoid the traditional overnight disappearance, or the more subtle urging to leave by kindly deans and psychiatric personnel. Only honesty is an offense, I realize, remembering the case I had heard of at Goucher. There was an incredible freshman girl who announced her lesbianism to the entire dormitory, was soon reported by her righteous neighbors and her "victim," a person thus redeemed whom the authorities soothed and sheltered. The offender will probably never go to college again, since her very enlightened parents have chosen to imprison her at home until she is 21 and has "learned better"—a whim which the law permits them. I wonder how odd college life might become if the response over every coed seduced by the local male talent would be to expel the chap—here's a double standard one had never considered before.

As I talk to these Vassar undergrads, I begin to feel the weight of their isolation, the guilt and the ostracism they live with every day, the oppression of this place as they must know it. It has been so hard that they cannot, dare not, accept our sympathy. "It hasn't been that bad," they insist. "A few people have been kind. Not everyone has put us down." Had they expected unanimity? And "coming out" has been beautiful, they insist, clutching after the individual joys of love to push back the enormity of social circumstances. "We won't be here next year anyway but in New York with our friends." Four will graduate. Only one, a junior, the girl who has worked hardest of all, is in a position to carry on the organization at Vassar, and she is not coming back: prefers New York. It emerged, too, that the intensity of political activity had caused her grades to fall, an opening for the gentle persuaders to advise her to drop out, take a year off, get herself together. It is clear that a year alone here would be unbearable.

We had talked ourselves into total despondency. There was clearly nothing left to say, because the affection, the respect, the compassion that I felt, I was too awkward to express well and they too farouche to receive. This was good-bye. We would not meet for breakfast in the morning. Coming back from the shower I noticed a position paper "The Woman-Identified Woman" (lesbianism and female oppression) bravely nailed to the door. Falling asleep, I felt the weight of the place, wondering at Barbara's puzzled exhaustion. Remembering my own history in guilt and shame, I recognized how this place could strangle you, tear away all recent assurance, the new world the Congress had promised—the urbanity, the permissiveness of New York. Next morning we couldn't wait to be on the road and away. Just before we left, one last phone call to the Vassar bunch—self-conscious and painful but loving under its gruffness.

Then off. We would go to Smith today. Breakfast at Howard Johnson's. The pancakes are superb and so's the weather, but as we leave for Smith we see an old etching of Vassar Female College in Ho-Jo's entry. Quaintly drawn, its red brick proud and new in the nineteenth century. Vassar Female College no longer exists. Neither does its Women's Liberation.

Many people in the movement would argue the greater expediency of staying away from the homosexual issue, keeping the group strong and intact. Remembering those five students, their suffering, their courage, I find I cannot agree. They took a course that made sense to them. It strikes me as a radical one, therefore one I must respect. One told me: "I came to Vassar, got myself laid at Yale and wondered why I did it. There comes a time when Woman's Liberation gets to you and you understand. And then a time came when loving each other made sense, too." Moreover, the issue itself is something all groups must deal with in time, just as the Congress had attempted to do. Vassar will have another Woman's Liberation next year. Freshman women will start it if no one else does. I wonder if it will live up to the tradition of its founders.

The road to Smith is glorious. There are flowers along the highway. We've turned in the first Avis, and Barbara is driving the second, a sports model. She relishes it. So blond, young, and beautiful, her mad vitality so humorous. A Smithie, she launches into her history at Smith. She loved it there, studied theater history with the best, was able to produce plays, to do what she liked. I think of the encouragement my students get at Barnard and realize I could never say I loved the factory where I was an undergraduate. Yet, simultaneous with hating and despising it, I suppose I really did love the girls' school I attended before the university. I begin to wonder why we love our own places—even when, like mine, they do so little to help us.

We drive right up to where the Smith Women's Lib group is sitting on the grass. We actually leap out and into the sun. They are glad to see us and they cheer. Embarrassing. I pick out friends from my last trip to Northampton in February—when I came up to speak to a large audience, drumming up interest in Women's Liberation. That time I talked tactics with the little group who were trying to organize. Today how many they seem, how untroubled is this serene group in contrast to the one we left at Vassar. There is a workshop on sexism and war. The strike has been imported by boys from Williams, Yale, Dartmouth, and Amherst—missionaries to instruct the broads at Smith in the rituals of Leftist politics. Boys give orders, girls obey.

When Women's Lib announced its workshop there was laughter and contempt. One hears the guys haranguing into bullhorns in other parts of the field, but the sound drifts across harmlessly. This group is together. After a while I think I can spot a few members of the faculty. One can tell two of them by age, another three by skirts. How pleasant that one can scarcely observe the mixture of castes.

We start to talk out an analysis of how sexual conditioning contributes soldiers to the state; the indoctrination and violence imposed on boys, the passive acceptance by females of their role as breeders providing new lives to die for country. We talk of Germany and how there it required feminism's death to get the female into line as baby maker and munitions plant worker.

The same pattern in Russia, too, where armaments took priority over people, while the creches and the collective housekeeping the Revolution had promised failed to materialize. World War II America was hardly different: war plant jobs and day care during the crisis, a rigged exodus from the labor market when it passed. Then the years of the "mystique." The neo-militarism of today's New Left male scarcely escapes us, his macho fantasy of guns and powder, only hypocrisy screaming for peace while lusting for the "right" war. We explore the connections between chauvinism and violence, sexism and racism, thinking of how only one in many of this war's deaths is military, the great bulk of its victims civilians— women and children. The fact that Sam regards us as beneath the contempt of his draft matters less when we know our identification is with the victims. We think of the American army brothels, government-sponsored, yet not staffed by WACS. Our boys need a racist fuck. Someone tells of the tags worn by the women in Saigon—small white circles tied around the neck—proof they've been fucked, washed out, inspected, certified fit for use again. War, rape, plunder, and fire are manly arts and Vietnam really American masculinity's accomplishment.

We break up to meet again after dinner. Meanwhile there's a leaflet to be done and a faculty reception to cope with. Barbara and I gather strength for the faculty, my onetime peer group. I can scarcely be called a member of Barnard's faculty any more—a fact my colleagues seemed to have grasped with an acumen swifter than my own. Hardly an undergraduate either, I seem, in spite of all, to be of that camp simply for lack of another. Only in the potential community of Columbia Women's Liberation where faculty, secretary, undergrad, and graduate student try to come together do I feel at ease.

We sit on a deck in the sun, nibbling sandwiches and lemonade, gazing at the outfits before us. Smith women wearing the male fist of the strike on their backs, stencilled on white shirts. It seems too appropriate, too obvious a symbol to have escaped notice.

At the reception, the faculty are impossible as always. They complain that strike classes will lack expertise. "How could French or economics contribute to one's understanding of Southeast Asia?" a professor demands, ignoring the value of the French press reports, or perhaps even imagining economy bears no relation to a war. A faculty member in chemistry informs me that his PhD makes him thoroughly competent in his field but prevents his involvement in any other—an illusion I admire, knowing my own degree failed somehow either to make me an expert at anything or to kill my interest in everything. The liberal faculty—both of them—return from a summit meeting to say there is no hope of faculty support for the strike. Smith, like Barnard, and probably every other school, is ruled by a super committee, variously called the Committee on Instruction, on Education, on Academic Affairs, or some such, and the local has just declared its superior neutrality by a vote of nine to one. Clearly, one must ignore the faculty for the time being.

Dinner is strike excitement—good stories, hasty exchanges of movement news between colleges, quick resumes of women's studies projected at Smith, the syllabus we're writing at Columbia. A young faculty member is there, the kind of junior who keeps students in school and the rest of us still teaching. We talk a while after dinner about what the movement has meant to us, to our students. She must leave now for faculty meeting. I can sense she dreads it. I know beforehand how she will wish to speak out and will be afraid, feeling the hostility, the very danger such statements bring for young women rare and lucky enough to have achieved this token status so unutterably precious to us: the chance to teach.

A bunch of us go downtown for an hour's bar break before the meeting at 8 PM. The place is full of conventioneers, drunk, lecherous, and edgy at the definite insubordination they sense in us. We in Women's Lib appear to give off special vibrations. When these types interrupt our conversation and impose themselves upon us, it is with more than ordinary banter and a quite particular bumptiousness. Asked not to intrude, then told to move on, they get ugly. We have a good talk with the waitresses, moving over to their stations since they are not permitted to sit. They deplore Cambodia with utter despair. A black waitress can count on nothing but God to stop the slaughter. Are they with the students? Yes, but we are powerless. We are all powerless. It may never end. They seem relieved, nevertheless, that someone still has some energy. We are elated by their good will. We like each other. The bartender begins to suspect our association.

The meeting was supposed to be a free-for-all rap on education, a favor for my research. Within five minutes it's a strike meeting. No one minds. The strike is immediate, as the spring of '68 taught us at Columbia: closing school to strike at reality is the most valid education one is likely to get. The circle on the floor expands as students drop in and join the conversation. Pat sits across from me, ever so carefully reasoning the ethics of student versus faculty, her Southern speech a wonder in itself, and the awe I feel before her flawless moral sensibility is very close to love.

Another girl who hadn't found Women's Lib relevant at all keeps asking splendidly exasperating, practical questions as to what we would actually do during the strike...until she is answered and we have composed a long, detailed list of activities whereby students may relate to the women in the Northampton area. This involves doing an unprecedented thing; it means seeing women as the people, those people whom student strikers—Smith women—wish to reach. We list the places women can be found—at home, in stores, laundries, beauty parlors, PTA's, in high school. Out of a shared, nearly ghetto-sharp cultural experience, we begin to realize we actually could reach other women. We can be fairly sure that housewives will let students in the door and talk to them if the students are simply other women talking to them as women, laying aside the rhetoric and relating as human beings simply outraged at murder.

A student named Robin comes back from the phone with an announcement we've all been waiting for: the faculty has finished meeting. They have not supported the strike. The student vote, compiled house by house and overwhelmingly in favor of a total strike, was not even announced to them. The senior class vote, nearly unanimous in favor of a strike even at the expense of a diploma, was not announced either. There is a good deal of resentment. I hear a voice, "Let's go see President Mendenhall," and we're off. It's raining shit and no one remembers an umbrella. Slugging along on a spontaneous visit to Big Daddy, we pass house after house, calling out our destination. Students seem to spring out of nowhere. It's hard to see, but when we arrive at the presidential mansion we're a multitude. We stand off for a moment. Three Williams boys suddenly jump out into the circular drive ahead of us— three figures in the dark telling us to stop, giving orders, running things even though they do not comprehend why we have come. Somehow this brings things to a head. The men are told to get back, we will go up to the house.

The rain is unbelievable; it's incredible that people can bear to stand in it. We try to sing to pull ourselves together—a clutch at morale. The bunch who called this action are a bit confused. Somehow 50 of us have put something in motion which has 500, perhaps 700 people in the downpour demanding that the president open his door and speak to us. There are a few ugly sounds. I worry if the crowd will get nasty. There can only be a score of males but their voices are violent and enormous. A fellow behind me continues to bellow "Shut up" to the whole crowd at bullhorn volume in an utterly bullying voice. He is told, firmly and politely, to keep quiet. Astonishment. More attempts to sing, this time for pacification rather than courage. Miraculously, the strike committee women make their way through the crowd and up to the door just as Mendenhall opens it.

The committee appears somewhat bewildered. As we are a spontaneous demonstration, they take a while to understand our demand for another faculty meeting where information on student attitudes is given out and reacted to honestly. This seems a good deal more than the committee would ever venture, but they realize the group cannot be put off. They enter to negotiate. We wait in the rain. We are too wet and too excited to sing now.

Someone calls my name, wanting me to harangue from the steps. I have no desire to grandstand here. So unnecessary, the idea seems ludicrous. Without having realized it, I've come to have a different notion of my job than I used to. It's not speechmaking now, just talking in small groups with the most committed. Coming in from the outside, full of the absurd optimism outsiders have, and where possible, here, as it wasn't at Vassar, contributing hope, putting the starch of such belief into the people there, acting as a catalyst to the catalyst group, at that moment when they'd really love to do something and aren't quite sure they can. When they're turned on, one stands back. This small group can organize others, who organize the rest.

Negotiations have reached a point. The door opens on the warm light and the dry. There *will* be a faculty meeting. Cheers. We demand a student representative. We are told that this is both "unheard of" and "unnecessary." The door closes. We are vocal in our discontent. The door opens again. There *will* be a student rep. I grin in the thunder, amused at how really vulnerable faculty and administration are, their only strength the fact that no one recognizes it. They are vulnerable most when unaccustomed to student power. Smith, like women's colleges in general, still spins on in bland innocence of the student bite.

The demonstration has succeeded beyond hope. I ask someone if it is often done here—visiting the president. "Once a year, about four or six of us might come with a grievance, arrive at a proper hour, sit politely, and be dismissed," I'm told. "Never, of course, like this." We leave, a bit dizzy with success we scarcely contemplated yet. Just before we decamp there is some Women's Lib sloganeering up in front. This is met with a groan or two—scattered hissing—but a new respect. The boys are quiet now, and as we walk off down the road they are advised to leave. Smith will have its own strike. The more intelligent comprehend that this is better really, more authentic. One or two will not let it drop till they are met with a moment's angry insult, which surprises them into listening. Gradually, both sides grow civil. I'm impressed by the demonstration's general shift in style and tone—from male belligerence to a firmness both more efficient and humane, more Smith than Jock, more woman's manner, even if its power is very new to women.

It's past midnight now, and there is still a statement to write for Women's Lib, something to be read before the whole school at the 9 AM rally. And as we begin putting it together from the day's notes, it emerges as a woman's thing to say about the war—an explanation of how Smith, acting on its own, asserting its identity as a women's college, responds to the repression at home, the atrocity over there. And when we're finished we notice we've never mentioned Women's Liberation—just women. We decide we'll leave it that way, depending on our own substance rather than the idiot image mass media has conjured up for our movement. Even though students identified with Women's Lib will read it at the meeting, it just might be heard for its own merit.

Strike headquarters has been telephoned for a spot on the agenda. They doubt they can find it. Our first delegation goes over. Probably there will be no time for us. The thought now occurs to us that *we* were the group who called the demonstration tonight and therefore we have a certain political clout which the committee would be absurd to ignore. We'll go across campus to visit them. During the long walk to Number 10 Prospect, climbing hills in the dark, I'm nearly dead with fatigue, wondering whether it is merely the dogged effort of a strike or the push of keeping up with youth which is defeating me.

At strike headquarters they behave as if protest were property, their property. We remind the committee that as volunteers they are in fact self-appointed. A good ten minutes of shouting before the statement can be read. One girl smirks; the rest listen. When it's finished several admit they agree. A few more volunteer that they are sympathetic to Women's Liberation, were even involved until the strike came along. We begin to get human with each other: in a few minutes an agreement is reached. We will be on tomorrow. We all leave together, discussing the selection of a democratically elected steering committee to involve everyone at Smith in the strike. A challenge had made the dead-tired committee defensive. No one seems to have thanked them before for the job they've done. They appear relieved at organized support, possibly even elated that the strike is Smith's now. The campus is all big quiet trees in a mist, a few lamps. Today's bossy masculine intervention has evaporated.

Some student has volunteered a splendid room for my use. I am past grudging Smith its comfort. There is the luxury of a bath, a shot of Scotch, half an hour for my obsessive lists and itinerary, privacy, and two hours of sleep. The past 17 hours have left me utterly exhausted, but I feel outrageously happy—until one thought brings it all down—there's a strike at Barnard now. That's my school. I should be there. Knowing my own Experimental College students, of course, I know there's nothing to worry about there. A special coeducational group who have won their maturity the hard way this year, educating me and themselves, I'm sure they'll be constructively involved. It's the rest of Barnard—the women undergraduates, the faculty. What's happening there now? It's Wednesday morning and I can't be in New York until Thursday. I fall asleep wondering what's right, knowing I can do more here yet balancing that against the greater obligation there.

The radio alarm to which students everywhere seem devoted fails me utterly. By 8:30 there's a contingent outside the door trying to wake me up. I have never been so painfully tired in my life. With infinite kindness they have found breakfast for me. Tactics and stage fright run together with toast and jam.

This is the last big meeting at John M. Green. All Smith is there—3,000 strong. It's a very different Smith from the radicals and Libbies I've known so far. Look around at the middle-class blandness packed tier on tier. It *does* seem possible Nixon's daughter could go here. Administration and faculty begin the meeting, secure in their power, confident on stage above masses of docile women. For a decade Smith has been raising its tone by firing women and faggots, achieving the magnificence of something like an 80 percent male faculty. Last night I could forgive Mendenhall's face-saving denial that he never knew the student vote was on his desk when he chaired the meeting. This morning the elaborations of parental righteousness grate on me as excessive self-indulgence. A Smithie's bitter remark at my first lunch there comes back: "We're the best ego trip these guys ever had."

After an hour the beams of authority dim somewhat. Coughing and squirming begin. It is clearly time for the student rally to be given back to the students. A statement or two is read. The response to the black women pleading for the Panthers is infuriating. This bunch seem hopeless; the chore of being a claque is getting harder. Then at last a girl rises to read our statement. Her voice is very fast and afraid, but gathering conviction and strangely moving as she races along—moving because her choked incoherence really signifies that she means what she says. The audience responds with silence beyond embarrassment. She has said the word "woman" several times; only "female" could have been more offensive (that was in the first draft). The one thing most women prefer to ignore is being forced upon them now. There is a contest of hisses and cheers. Finally, considerable applause, but still at odds with the booing.

Then strange things begin to happen. Women who have nothing to do with Women's Lib begin to shout for Smith's own strike—"Let the guys get off campus." A women's strike smells of crummy pacifism to radical girlfriends, feminine wishy-washy. To the daughters of suburbia it just seems indecent, yet it does have more appeal than the macho Left whom their common sense ways detested.

More rhetoric and talking up, a very healthy phenomenon. Then the huge place begins to throb. A chant of "Strike, strike, strike." Efforts on the stage to turn this off. Then, by a brilliant tactic, another student rally is called for after lunch, at one, just after faculty meeting. So the faculty must come and face *that* rally and say what they've done. Smithies are learning at last how to teach their teachers.

As we pour out of the building, regrouping for an instant to say good-bye, I feel a wrench at leaving now. It still feels shaky but my job's over. If anything's going to happen, it will happen now.

Three days later a student named Cindy brings the news. She's wonderfully incongruent as a representative of a ladies' college, here in my Bowery studio, full of hilarious poor white stories of North Carolina mountain kin, themselves wise and humorous enough to laugh at their booze and incest. And she already understands both the hope and the vulgar Snopecist decline of her own parents' generation which has fetched her way up to Smith. She's radiant. Women's Lib could pull it off, could get out in front of the strike and make it work, as someone had suggested in that first meeting on the grass. Having observed the political apathy on women's campuses all year, which, except for the exodus on weekends, is probably their most depressing characteristic, such activism had seemed only a chimera, however logical may be the proposition that only an issue as solidly their own as Women's Liberation could ever politicize these seminaries. "The strike is beautiful," she says. "We have a place on the Steering Committee." "And Smith's Women's Lib has five hundred members now." I remember the strike chant filling John M. Green and realize that in its 120 years as a women's college Smith had never had anything so real of its own, so alive and to the point.

Listening to Cindy's talk, amidst the confusion of entertaining guests while packing and ironing for another trip, I begin to realize how much of all this applies to me as well. For not till Smith probably had I ever tasted politics or seen power working for people. And my new striped pants on the ironing board, devastated in Mendenhall's rain, seem such a small exchange for such knowledge, they embarrass me as much as did the man himself that next morning when he left the rally. The new care in his face came as a rebuke to the outlaw I've become. Ten years of faculty membership, even at, or below instructor's rank, should have filed me elsewhere. A series of accidents: our own '68 Columbia, getting sacked once or twice, the fire of this war, and at each step of the way the Women's Movement over and above all the rest — these things have all conspired to produce in me a person so out of control as to believe each moment's teaching a challenge to integrity between moral choices too big to compromise. By watching some who did, I have discovered that the cost of keeping a job can be exorbitant. To work now, to do the job, will have to mean being ready to go at any moment, one's bag always packed.

Women's Lib and the Women's Colleges

By Caroline Bird

Women's liberation isn't as big at women's colleges as it is at some coeducational universities, but it raises issues that can't be settled by adding a staff gynecologist or a course in the history of women. The search for a new female identity strikes the women's colleges at their ideological core: why a separate college for women to begin with?

Women's colleges, including those that have recently admitted men, can be classified according to why they were founded for women only:

First there are the Catholic women's colleges, founded to educate girls while protecting their chastity. Nuns administered sex segregation in the service of a tradition that prescribes two inflexible biologically based roles for women: ritual celibacy or repeated childbearing. As such, these colleges are the ideological bastions of resistance to women's liberation. Paradoxically, however, those that have joined the current movement to reform the Catholic church have produced some of our most radical feminists. Nuns like Sister Joel Read, president of Alverno College in Milwaukee, are ecumenical about sisterhood. They want to broaden the bond between women in orders to include all women everywhere. Alverno does everything that women activists want women's colleges to do. It has day care centers, women's studies, research on women, political action on behalf of women, community services for women.

Next—and very numerous—are the "finishing school" type women's colleges which are typical of the South. They are frankly sexist in origin, founded to prepare girls for marriage and motherhood, or failing a suitable match, self support in a "feminine" job such as school teaching. The response of their students to women's liberation has lagged in part because they have attracted students from conservative families who see these colleges as a haven from campus turbulence and the sexual revolution.

But the "finishing school" colleges are hard hit by changing styles of marriage, which make coeducational colleges better places to find a husband for those who still regard marriage as a primary vocation. And some of them are desperate enough to pitch the "female haven" appeal in rhetoric that co-opts the women's liberation "line." A recruiting brochure issued by the Southern Association of Colleges for Women promises that at a woman's college "you can be your own woman, playing the dating game on your own terms... you do not have to stand in line behind men to use expensive scientific equipment, computer terminals, studios, the pool, tennis courts, or the gymnasium."

Finally, there are the colleges of the Northeast, the academically rigorous Ivy League Seven Sisters—Vassar, Smith, Wellesley, Mt. Holyoke, Bryn Mawr, Radcliffe and Barnard—all of which now admit male students. Philosophically they are the antithesis of the "finishing school" colleges: they were founded not to prepare women for marriage, motherhood or a special feminine role, but to give them the Harvard or Yale education denied them during the nineteenth century on the ground of their sex. For many years—possibly as late as the 1930s—they offered the most exacting college education a woman could get. Because they educated the movement's ideologues—Betty Friedan and Gloria Steinem went to Smith, I went to Vassar—they should have cradled the new demand for sex equality. Instead, women's liberation has been an embarrassment to which they have reluctantly been forced to react. (See Kate Millett, "Women and War," page 195.)

The record is startling. To check it quickly, I counted the references to colleges among the hundreds of events and statements in the Chronology appended to *The Rebirth of Feminism*, the exhaustive history of the new movement by Judith Hole and Ellen Levine published in 1972 by Quadrangle Books. Between 1961 and the fall of 1971, some things worthy of inclusion happened at or to the following institutions, in chronological order of first mention: University of Washington, University of Chicago, Grinnell, Cornell, University of California at Berkeley, Columbia University, New York University Law School, Harvard University, University of Michigan Law School, Princeton University, San Diego State College, City College of New York.

There were only two references to women's colleges:

May 9, 1966: Sarah Lawrence College President Esther Raushenbush and Radcliffe College President Mary Bunting charged that American universities fail to recognize that many college-trained women want both families and careers.

January 1971: Goucher College (Maryland) offers course for women titled "Nuts and Bolts in Contemporary Society." Students learn small appliance repair, carpentry, plumbing and electronics.

This dismal record of the women's colleges was confirmed when I made a similar list of the institutional affiliations of witnesses before the 1970 House hearings held by Congresswoman Edith Green on discrimination against women. People came or were quoted from the universities of Wisconsin, Buffalo, Chicago, California, Illinois and Maryland; from Columbia, Carnegie-Mellon, Purdue, Cornell and Kansas State Teachers College. Victoria Schuck, professor of political science at Mt. Holyoke, and Alice Rossi of Goucher were the only witnesses from colleges founded for women.

Women's liberation first attracted national attention in 1968 when radical New York women picketed the Miss America contest in Atlantic City and got televised attention by threatening to throw their brassieres in Freedom Trash Baskets. (For the record, they didn't.) It erupted that year on the big coeducational campuses, often as an offshoot of radical movements for civil rights, peace in Vietnam or student power. From these campus hotbeds the new movement spread and so came ultimately to the women's colleges.

At Vassar, as well as at her sister colleges, there has long been a kind of intellectual disdain for the whole subject of the special qualities and duties of women. Because of this, the first consciousness-raising groups were small and so ill-understood by the administration that according to one possibly apocryphal story, President Alan Simpson didn't know there was such a thing. On being asked whether Vassar had them, he decided to investigate personally only to discover that he was not welcome because he was male.

Nor is it only male administrators who respond coolly to the new movement's unabashed emphasis on femininity. Many of the single women scholars who set the tone of the Ivy League women's colleges are now nearing retirement, and they patronize the young activists. Like a majority of women on most cross-sectional polls of opinion, they applaud the goals of women's liberation but deplore its tactics. "You can't expect us to get excited about the need for upgrading women," the dean of Mt. Holyoke remarked: "We've been saying this all along"—and, she implied, more temperately.

Sometimes it looks like a generation gap, at other times a difference of personal style or even semantics. But the gulf is as frustrating as if it were on substantive issues and is well worth exploring. In 1970, for instance, the fledgling women's liberation group at Vassar protested that the Vocational Bureau was not actively "demanding" jobs for graduates commensurate with their education. "The Vocational Bureau must stop telling women who want to be doctors that they ought to become nurses instead," a student leader demanded.

The director of the Vocational Bureau, a dedicated and skilled personnel officer, indignantly denied that she had ever discouraged any student from a medical career. Jane Johnson and I were Vassar classmates and I can't imagine her ever doing such a thing—or forgiving anyone for distorting a fact to make a phrase. "We haven't been talking about equal opportunity all these years, we've been doing something about it!" she complained. Jane's tact and gentle persuasion of employers reluctant to take on women has simply not been credited by the most recent crop of student activists—nor the fact that she and many of the rest of us negotiated sexual politics to lead liberated lives long before Kate Millett analyzed them.

How come the misunderstanding? I shall contend that the answer lies less in fundamental ideological differences than in the unexpected interaction of trends such as the fluctuations in birth and marriage rates since World War II, the sexual revolution of the sixties, coeducation and changes in the socioeconomic origins of Ivy League women that occurred when the prosperity of the fifties flooded them with so many applicants that only highly motivated intellectuals got into them.

What happened, I think, is that the Seven Sisters did a right-about face following World War II. Up to that point they had been dominated by social reformers, dedicated to androgyny or minimizing sex differences, and hopelessly upper class. The Old Feminists claimed that "Women are people" and won the vote for women by tactics more shocking and more dangerous to them personally than the unladylike attention-getting devices of "women's lib."

After World War II, they were overshadowed by people who were establishment, sexist (*"vive la différence"*), and concerned with making college a place where daughters of self-made fathers could learn how to meet and marry desirable husbands. Their code was an endearing version of traditional sex roles I have called New Masculinism because it prescribes that women serve men not by performing fixed duties such as baking cherry pies (that's Old Masculinism), but by responding sensitively to the changing needs of business or politics. New Masculinism produced such women as Mary Lindsay (Vassar '47), who devotes her considerable talents to providing whatever ambience is needed by John Lindsay (Yale '44), the former mayor of New York City. The Lindsays are typical of many Vassar-Yale marriages of their time.

During the fifties, the Ivy League women's colleges came to be known as the "Seven Sisters." What *McCall's* called "togetherness" and Betty Friedan called the "feminine mystique" invaded the curriculum. At one point, child study became the biggest undergraduate major at Vassar, and young families were installed as house fellows in residence units to provide a "warmer, more home-like" atmosphere. At Mills College in California, fondly known as the "Vassar of the West," President Lynn White designed a "truly feminine" higher education for women in child care, homemaking and such womanly vocations as occupational therapy, medical library work and domestic science.

The shift is not something I am making up out of whole cloth by hindsight. I was so surprised at the new domesticity that I returned from a visit to my daughter (Vassar '57) to write an article for the now defunct *American Mercury* on the "New Look at Vassar." I felt that the New Masculinism of the student body had something to do with the increase in the proportion of students coming from public high school and families with less income and education than in the more rigidly class-and-income-stratified days before World War II. There is a great deal of sociological evidence that upper-class women have always been freer from domestic obligations and the constraints of "femininity" than women who were brought up with fewer privileges.

During the fifties, "good" women's colleges had a much higher proportion than before of students whose parents were able and ambitious to give their children a better education than they themselves had enjoyed. Marriage had always been the way for women to "make it," but there seemed parents now who were quite anxious for their children to succeed. During the fifties, millions of families moved up the socioeconomic scale and brought with them their old high valuation of domesticity and their traditional concern that "boys should be boys" and "girls should be girls" with no crossing of boundaries.

Meanwhile, early and almost universal marriage and motherhood had consequences for the faculty as well as the students. Fewer women went on to graduate school, and those who did were more apt to become encumbered with a family. Husbands and children made it hard for them to teach in one-sex college communities, and married women scholars followed their husbands. Young men—often with unaspiring wives—were freer to move, and they began to replace the older feminists at the lower faculty ranks of the women's colleges.

No one was immediately alarmed at the invasion. New Masculinists were glad to see a more "natural" mixture of the sexes. Old Feminists insisted that it didn't matter because competence was more important than sex. Still, Marion Tait, Vassar's dean emeritus of faculty, insists that the college always preferred women candidates to men. "The trouble in those days was that we simply could not find them," she recalls. "Few women scholars were being produced, and times were so good that those who were found it easier than formerly to get jobs elsewhere. Our sex ratio got badly out of hand."

But during the sixties, the scene shifted again. The whole society grew less marriage-oriented, and so did the Seven Sisters. The pace of social mobility slowed: fewer parents were as anxious for their daughters to make "good" marriages. The continuing crunch on admissions meant that more and more Seven Sisters undergraduates were superb scholars bent on graduate school. The pill and the sexual revolution were changing the terms of man-woman relations and reducing the urgency to marry young. More initially chose coeducational schools where the new "natural" relations between men and women supposedly prevailed. And it was in these coeducational schools that women's liberation first appeared.

Why there first? Bernice Sandler, who pioneered suing universities for discrimination as government contractors, thinks that "the enemy was clearer" at the coeducational schools like Cornell or San Diego State College, which women forced to pioneer women's studies courses. There women were surrounded by men who regarded them as date bait or potential wage earners ready to drop out of college and support a male through school if the relationship became serious.

Fewer of them came from upper-class families with a tradition of personal choice of life style. Aristocratic traditions of freedom and autonomy were not as central to the traditions and institutions of these big coeducational colleges as they have always been at smaller, private, historically one-sex colleges in the Northeast.

At the coeducational colleges, women were often diverted into courses of study regarded as "feminine" or leading to feminine occupations such as teaching, and the women employed by the university were doing low prestige, underpaid "women's jobs." So women students there couldn't escape daily reminders of the special and inferior role of women, and it moved the egalitarians among them to revolt.

When Betty Friedan talked about the feminine mystique, coeds at big universities knew what she was talking about. At Vassar, on the contrary, she was coolly received. Five years ago students there came to hear her out of intellectual curiosity, but they didn't take what she had to say personally. Each student interested enough to listen thought she would find some way around the limitations of the mystique. *She* was not going to marry and move to the suburbs and rot. And even if she didn't expect to remain single, as some of her teachers had, her daily experience at college reminded her that there were options. If she married, it would be on her own terms; and if those terms were domestic, it would be because she deliberately chose them in preference to other possible life styles. Coeds for the most part did not enjoy this luxury. They knew they weren't free, and the activists among them joined the new movement.

Policymakers in coeducational institutions had few defenses against their attacks. They had known that race discrimination was wrong, but about sex discrimination they had to be educated. Some of them learned. "The fact is that higher education has been institutionalized on a male basis," Alan Pifer, president of the Carnegie Corporation, told the Southern Association of Colleges and Schools in 1971: "The introduction of women into its positions of power upsets the system and causes difficulties." It's hard to imagine anyone in Pifer's position perceiving in 1965 the institutionalization of sex role as a problem.

Policymakers in the women's colleges were less vulnerable because they weren't so innocent. They knew that women weren't really equal even in academia, but they were New Masculinists whose attitudes were shaped by the sexist fifties. They accepted the situation, or hoped for gradual improvement in the lot of women in the distant future. When I interviewed Mary Bunting and Esther Raushenbush in 1966 for *Born Female*, both were as defensive and fearful of quotation as liberals charged with racism who aren't quite sure how they feel about Negroes personally. And just as self-deluding liberals early cited the many successful blacks as evidence that the blacks could make it if they tried, so policymakers in women's colleges cited women achievers as evidence that any woman could do anything she wanted to do if she would only shut up and work at it. From this aristocratic point of view, expressed articulately in Midge Decter's "The Liberated Woman" (*Commentary*, October 1970), the women activists could be dismissed as uncouth and ineffective whiners. Things weren't that bad, the Seven Sisters policymakers said to each other—and most importantly, of course, to themselves.

What they didn't like to admit is that the women they can cite to prove that sex barriers can be surmounted turn out to be a singularly well-heeled and socially privileged lot. Indira Gandhi made it to the top as the daughter of India's independence hero. A high proportion of U.S. women legislators broke into politics as widows of politically powerful men. And we might never have had woman suffrage at all if rich women like Mrs. O. H. P. Belmont had not been able to support the fight with capital inherited from males. After suffrage was won, the money went to the League of Women Voters, which promptly adopted the well-bred disregard for the de facto subordination of women which is the establishment posture of the Seven Sisters to this day.

As the sixties progressed, it was obvious that the Seven Sisters weren't with it. Alarmed that they might lose their attraction for the most highly motivated college-bound women, all of them considered getting men on campus. The remedy was enthusiastically promoted by the men who had been hired on their faculties in the fifties. Some had acquired tenure and influence and were openly talking among themselves about the need to get rid of the "old girls" just ahead of them. Many frankly admitted that they wanted to teach men.

This was the state of affairs in the Seven Sisters in 1968 when the women's liberation movement appeared, a cloud on the horizon the size of a man's hand. Occupied with coeducation, administrators at first paid little attention to the groups on campus. Even as late as 1970, Alan Simpson was soliciting opinions from faculty and alumnae on whether women were as valid a focus for study as the blacks, and if so, whether women's studies should be segregated in a special center or reflected in existing course content. Bryn Mawr ultimately recognized the new interest by inviting Kate Millett to teach a special course on women.

This school year there are more courses and fewer doubts. The number of courses qualifying as women's studies has almost doubled. Bernice Sandler, executive associate of the Association of

Women's Colleges, has counted seven hundred all over the country, and the women's colleges now have their share. Suzanne Keller is professor of sociology at Princeton, but her somewhat guarded response could be duplicated among women scholars across the entire country: "Women's studies? Last year I was against them, but this year I think I am for them."

Barnard is launching a Women's Center with a library on women, career planning facilities and a dozen courses with titles such as "The Role of Women in Modern Economic Life" and "Images of Women in Literature." Vassar has six courses on women, one of which is "Women in American Law and Politics" taught by a woman added to the political science department in part for that purpose. But more is going on than gets into the catalogue. The political scientist who teaches the course on civil liberties doesn't talk about the civil liberties of women, but his students remind him of the omission by electing to do term papers on the topic.

Since the early 1970s women's liberation has become a permanent feature on all Seven Sisters campuses. Male administrators are under fire. There is general agreement now that no man can be expected in the future to get the presidency of any of the Seven Sisters without facing articulate opposition on the ground of his sex. During the sixties, Alan Simpson replaced Sarah Blanding at Vassar, Charles DeCarlo replaced Esther Raushenbush at Sarah Lawrence, and in 1969, Harris L. Wofford, Jr., replaced Katharine McBride at Bryn Mawr. Academic women say that Wofford is the "last male replacement." Smith chose Jill Conway to succeed Thomas Mendenhall upon his retirement.

There's also a new sensitivity about sex ratio on the faculty. While many have a majority of women on the faculty, Wellesley is the only one of the seven with more tenured females than males. Most campuses now have special studies under way to see whether women applicants are getting a fair shake, and the percentages hired are passed around like major league scores.

Most young college women take the objectives of women's liberation for granted. They now assume they have control over their own bodies, access to any kind of work they want or any life style they wish. The fair question is how many of them are joining women's liberation as a movement, wearing feminist buttons, seeing putdowns all around them, joining consciousness-raising sessions, mounting protests against the firing of women or for day care centers and abortion clinics. More are doing such things each year, and some are emotionally involved because they feel men have been "invading" the campus.

"The first men weren't a problem," a Vassar student testified at open hearings held by the trustees. "We could absorb them into the female scene, and we stood a good chance of sensitizing them to the needs of women. But now that there are so many of them, they're taking over!" Others wonder whether the presence of men has diluted scholarship support of women. Administrators worry about issues that would never have arisen if there were no men around to measure sex equality, such as whether women students need "protecting" and if so whether male or female guards should be hired to do it.

The consciousness of the men who have pioneered coeducation at women's colleges is being raised quite as painfully as the consciousness of the women. At Vassar and at Sarah Lawrence there were fears that the first men wouldn't be as bright as the women. They were—and in addition their interests are proving not so different from the women's, as some of the young male faculty may have hoped. "I was surprised to find that the men are just as interested in, say, peace, as the women students," a male Vassar professor commented. "I guess I was thinking like a male chauvinist," he added, demonstrating his new-found sensitivity.

Plumbing and pregnancy have not presented the insuperable problems middle-aged administrators foresaw. Young men and women have had no trouble in sharing bathroom facilities in dormitories, and anyone so old-fashioned as to worry about premarital sex is apt to be rewarded with a patronizing smile from undergraduates. But noise! Ah, that's another matter.

One-sex dormitories have been getting noisier for years, but coeducation makes it worse. Women who opt for women's dormitories say that men are just too noisy. But men think that the women are noisy, too. Coeducational dormitories have required some of the accommodations of marriage, and for some the adjustment has been negative.

Most students and faculty accept coeducation as inevitable, but whether at Princeton or Vassar, the men seem to be happier about it than the women. Mt. Holyoke, Smith, Wellesley and Bryn Mawr are glad that they can have undergraduate men from neighboring colleges on campus without admitting them to full student citizenship by granting them degrees. They want to remain essentially women's colleges.

So do Barnard and Radcliffe. Barnard students aren't sure they want closer relations with Columbia College across Broadway. "The courtship is over!" an exasperated Columbia proponent of union declared in a recent debate. "Barnard has to realize that it's rape or nothing!" The remark was reported by a Barnard woman as an example of the aggressive, sexist attitudes from which Barnard women want to protect themselves by remaining separate.

The Seven Sisters were founded to help women overcome the discrimination against them. In the late 1960s, most students and faculty didn't think women needed a one-sex haven any more. Now they are not so sure. "While the conditions that historically justified the founding of women's colleges have clearly changed to some extent," the Mt. Holyoke Trustees Committee on Coeducation concluded in 1969, "they remain in the less tangible but still potent areas of attitude, feeling, spirit. There remain, in short, cultural reasons justifying the existence of colleges primarily for women."

Similar reasoning dominated the April 1971 Smith College report that recommended against granting Smith degrees to men and for limiting the number of men on campus. They were influenced, they say, because "at the present time, when the status and roles of women in American society are being reexamined with a view to their improvement, an important option that should remain open to women is attendance at a college of the highest caliber in which women are unquestionably first-class citizens." Women's liberation has raised the consciousness of the "old girls" who dealt with discrimination by denying it existed.

Vassar admits men to degrees and is moving toward a 50-50 sex ratio in 1975, but Alan Simpson promises that this won't mean "male-dominated coeducation": "We are going to do everything in our power to make this a college where the sexes are on a footing of genuine equality and where the women are not pushed around by the men." A vocal minority at Vassar dissents. "It is not the purpose of a college to be a microcosm of society." Nancy Schrom, a recent graduate now teaching at the college testified, "Vassar needs to be dedicated to feminism."

Most feminists, including myself, believe that men and women ought to be able to live together on an equal basis. Most of us are leary of quotas. We're delighted to see how many young people can live comfortably on coeducational campuses without parietal rules. But consciousness raising has shown that sex integration isn't as easy or "natural" as it looked. Women's liberation has further demonstrated that liberation from sex stereotypes is one of the things that women are going to have to do by and for themselves, and where better than in a women's college founded for that express purpose?

Why Women Go Back to College

By Pat Durchholz and Janet O'Connor

Mabel Davis is a trim, energetic woman of 44 who lives in a mid-size city. One fall Mabel sent her youngest child off to a prestigious Eastern university and enrolled herself in the local community college. With some hard work, Mabel expects to hang her bachelor's degree on the wall when her son does.

Mabel Davis (a fictitious name) shares one characteristic with an ever-growing number of women over 25 in the United States today: they are going back to college, or enrolling for the first time. In some publicly supported colleges, these women make up as much as 10 percent of the student body. Furthermore, they are being greeted with mounting enthusiasm by harried administrators trying to fill seats left empty by the wandering and decreasing numbers of young people.

Although some research has been done on the characteristics of these women, we found that there had been no research to connect their decisions to return to college with any one factor. We wanted to find out why these women return to college and what they plan to do with their education.

We thought that the factors influencing a woman's

decision to return to college would be complex. Many women face certain social barriers to this decision: their friends or relatives may think that career aspirations are unfeminine; they may be told that they would be neglecting their families by pursuing a degree and later a job. Even in the college classroom the mature woman may meet opposition: younger students and faculty may consider her an outsider with goals less serious than theirs—the suburban matron looking for a change from her diet of soap operas and envelope stuffing for local politicians.

Since the number of women seeking continuing education is increasing, we reasoned that their motivation would have to be quite strong to overcome these barriers. The mature woman must have good reasons for putting up with criticism, misunderstanding, and outright hostility in order to spend her time in the classroom. And it seemed to us that if the mature woman is to be accepted as a serious student with a valid career goal, data to substantiate that image would have to be collected.

We designed a study for the purpose of determining just why women are returning to college to continue their education. Are they in fact just looking for a new way to spend their leisure time or are they seeking career training? We sent a questionnaire to a random sample of 245 women who were continuing their education at the Clifton and Raymond Walters campuses of the University of Cincinnati. These women were undergraduates, 25 years old or older, and attending day school. The results of the survey are based on 186 responses, 75.9 percent of the sample.

Our questionnaire (sent out in January 1973) asked why a woman had returned to college, what her degree goals were, what her class standing was compared with the number of years since she had returned to college, how significant her student role was in her life, what her career aspirations were, and what plans she had for working after graduation.

The women listed these reasons for returning to school: 35.4 percent to prepare for employment; 30.3 percent to fulfill a need or desire for education or achievement; 25.3 percent to facilitate personal growth; 4.5 percent to promote independence; and 4.5 percent for stimulation.

Forty-seven percent of the women hoped to obtain degrees beyond the BA. Only 10.8 percent wished to obtain doctorates, but 36.6 percent were working for a master's. Close to 35 percent were working for a bachelor's degree and 10.8 percent for the associate degree.

Although 54.8 percent of the sample were attending classes only part-time, the women tended to have the appropriate class standing for the number of years they had been back in college. For example, 62.9 percent of all the first-year students were freshmen; 47.7 percent of the fourth-year students were seniors. This suggests that the women were making steady progress toward their degree goals and that the majority would earn a bachelor's degree after four or five years.

When asked, "Is your student role a significant one in your life?," 55.5 percent of the women answered "very significant." Over 22 percent said it was "moderately important" and 19.2 percent called it "an interesting dimension." Only 2.7 percent answered that it was "not really" important.

When asked if they planned to work after graduation, 71.6 percent of the women replied "definitely." Over 63 percent had returned to college with specific careers or job goals in mind. Their plans to work were influenced by their financial needs; but even so, 41.9 percent of those who said that they did not need to work for financial reasons were still planning to do so.

The University of Cincinnati's records show that the population from which our sample was drawn earned excellent grades. During the period in which our sample was selected, both full- and part-time students had B averages.

When asked, "What was going on in your life that prompted you to become a student?," and whether this constituted a personal or family crisis, only 23.7 percent of the women said that a crisis precipitated their return to college. The questionnaire did not define "crisis" because we wanted to obtain unstructured responses. We found that a husband's death, divorce, financial problems, and a search for identity were among the crises these women faced.

A change in their family's life style brought some of the women back to college. For example, some women came back when their children were all in school, others when their children had all left home. Some women said, "My husband finished his degree and now it's my turn." Some felt that "it was now or never."

Other studies that have been done on women who return to college stress that they are dedicated students. Our data indicate that the women in our sample were similar to women at other universities or colleges. They have high educational goals. They earn high grades. They consider their student role important. They carry course loads that enable them to earn a bachelor's degree in four or five years. And they are oriented to employment after college.

The positive aspects of mature women returning to college to prepare for a professional life are numerous. Our fast-changing society will have a new resource to tap in a job market that is demanding educated and flexible workers. A new supply of productive and trained talent is becoming available for the end of this century when some population experts see the productive labor talent diminishing.

And in these years when the numbers of 18- and 19-year-old women entering college are leveling off, returning women students may provide career role models for younger women. As a matter of fact, in answer to a question about their children's attitudes toward their return to college, 77.5 percent of our respondents said that their children's attitudes were favorable or very favorable.

However, the problems of women returning to college may require a good deal of attention. For instance, while the market for women graduates with business and technical degrees is now strong, many mature women are still concentrating their studies in teaching and liberal arts, where job opportunities are decreasing. In our sample, 25.3 percent of the women were enrolled in the Teachers College on the Clifton campus where they were training for the already overcrowded profession of elementary and secondary teaching. An additional 27.5 percent of the women listed liberal arts majors, and many of them planned to earn graduate degrees so they could teach at the college level. Opportunities here would be slim also. Counselors and advisers are needed to inform these women about the job market and future trends.

Another issue is how barriers that are preventing even more women from returning to college can be removed—assuming it is agreed that this is a desirable trend. Certainly adequate child-care facilities would be a boon to both women students and women university employees. But there may be more serious obstacles. When asked what their husbands' attitudes were to their return to college, 76.3 percent of our respondents replied that their husbands' attitudes were either favorable or very favorable. But how many women who wish to re-enter college are not doing so because of their husbands' opposition? If a husband is opposed to his wife's education or career goals, needs such as help with child care and housework can become serious problems.

Even more serious, in most states if a woman's husband does not consent to share his income for her tuition or will not sign a student loan application, she will not be able to go to college. She will be ineligible for financial aid because of her husband's earnings. Unless the woman has an independent income, she may be forced to spend her life in an economic childhood.

These are serious problems which must be dealt with if we are to take advantage of the talents these highly motivated and intelligent persons have to offer. Leaders in education, government, and business should be seriously considering how they can help the mature woman attain her goals. She's not just "getting older." As our study shows, she's determined to get a better education.

A "Second Chance" Program for Women

By Elisabeth Hansot

A *New Yorker* cartoon shows an ample, middle-aged woman huddled in the corner of her living-room sofa clutching a tear-stained handkerchief. Her balding husband, hands shoved deep into trouser pockets, stands to one side gazing at her with a baffled, weary expression. The caption reads, "A course at the New School—that's your answer to everything." The cartoon is prominently displayed in the crowded offices of the Human Relations Work-Study Center, an interdisciplinary department of the New School for Social Research.

The New School for Social Research, at the northern edge of Greenwich Village in New York City, was founded in 1919 by a handful of dissident Columbia University professors to offer evening courses for adults who wanted to choose what they wanted to learn without having to take prescribed programs. It was characterized recently in the *New York Times* as an institution "that has spent its first fifty years trying to cope with the problem of what to do for an encore." The Human Relations Center is part of that encore. It prides itself on being the oldest (twenty years) continuing education center for women in the country.

Since its creation, the Center has changed its character dramatically from a leisure- and volunteer-activity orientation to a no-nonsense commitment to devising ways for women to get back into the mainstream. Ruth Van Doren, the director of the Center, has a clear sense of the need it fills. "The middle-class woman is suffering, just as the poverty woman, for lack of productive work," she says. "And frequently she has been made to feel that the work incentive itself is shameful—that it reflects badly on her husband's earning capacity or on her own resourcefulness as a 'homemaker.' But this is changing. Women want an identity outside the family, and I hear an undertone in their voices that says, 'I will do this for me, now.'"

The Human Relations Center has about 1,700 adults enrolled each semester and about 3,500 each year; 95 percent of them are women. The typical student is a well-to-do urban or suburban woman (50 percent commute from the suburbs) anywhere from her early twenties through her late sixties. She is married with 2.5 children and motivated by the desire to get back into what she envisions as the mainstream of life. In good part because their needs are undramatic and not easily categorized, Ms. Van Doren describes these women as "forgotten Americans."

"The professional woman knows how to get what she wants," she says. "But a lot of the women who come here need encouragement, support and sensible advice. A woman may be in her thirties, recently separated and trying to make it for the first time on her own. Or she may be in her late forties or fifties with her children finally grown up and with time to begin to think about her own future. She probably has had some college study and may have worked a bit on the side, but she hasn't really had important work experience. Her husband could be a salesman or run his own business; he earns a decent living and she doesn't have to work. Scholarships for this sort of woman are nonexistent and there is little in the line of serious counseling. She needs trained help to focus herself, find out what she can realistically do as well as what she wants to do and, even more important, what is available to be done."

The Center faculty, in the New School tradition, are almost all part-time teachers working in the professional areas in which they teach. They include among their number a senior vice president of a public relations firm who teaches a course on women moving up; a former employment-agency owner and personnel director who teaches a vocational workshop designed to inform women about career possibilities and teach them how to prepare resumes and handle job interviews; a psychotherapist giving a course on future human relations; and a community medicine instructor from Mt. Sinai Hospital who gives one of the series of intensive training programs in the community services area. (Community service courses enroll 300 of the Center's 1,700 students each semester.) The faculty, busy with their own careers, create in their classrooms a sense of urgency and involvement that maintains the Center at a safe distance from the self-indulgent, desultory "teatime" atmosphere found in some women's programs.

That sense of urgency is reinforced by the work-study format requiring students to be active outside the classroom and breaking down the time-honored separation between learning and doing. The keys to this approach are the enrollment options and the course variety available to the student. A woman is allowed to audit courses before formally enrolling for credit. As her interests develop, she can go into the certificate program, then on to a BA. The sequence isn't rigid; a noncredit student can move into the BA program and degree students into the certificate program.

A frequently travelled route for the returning housewife at the Center is to enroll in the certificate program. The certificate program is aimed specifically at the woman who has been out of school for some time and is designed to allow her to explore new vocational interests or to prepare for advanced academic training. The program consists of ten semester courses, selected partly from the Center's interdisciplinary courses and partly from courses offered by the New School, and an action project undertaken in the last year of study. The program allows a woman to tailor her studies to her special interests and pursue them at her own pace. Theoretically, a highly motivated woman could achieve this result on her own, but in fact for many who have been away from school for a long period, the discipline of a set of related and sequential courses is an important test of their abilities to achieve self-determined goals.

Central to the certificate program is the project seminar, undertaken in the final year. Its object is to capitalize on the student's ability to design and complete an independent action project and present a critical evaluation of the work. Projects vary widely in nature and scope. One woman initiated a craft program in a new Montessori school. Another helped Mexican artists present a series of exhibitions of their batik and silk-screening process. A 70-year-old woman organized art classes for the Widows' Consultation Service in New York; another set up a replica of the Human Relations Center on Long Island. Summing up the program, Ms. Van Doren says: "Think of learning as a process, a process on which you eventually have to act. What we want to measure is the growth of the student's capacity to act, and that is also a measure of her productivity."

The certificate course sets no time limit for its completion although the Center recommends taking at least one course a term. The drop-out rate is 60-70 percent, a source of considerable satisfaction for the director. "When they drop out of this program, they drop into a job or into a BA program and that's what we're looking for," remarks Ms. Van Doren. "The Center is here for women who use it as a tool for a more satisfying engagement with life, not for degrees or certificates."

Just recently the Center has persuaded the New School to accept the certificate for thirty points of credit toward a BA degree. Ms. Van Doren is ambivalent about this achievement. The pressure for credit comes from students who want the status of a degree and the mobility it permits from one job to another. Moreover, many certificate graduates work in health, social welfare or in the schools, where state and civil service requirements frequently make credentials a necessity to avoid dead-end jobs. "Before we asked for credit," says Ms. Van Doren, "we used the certificate to try to break down the credentials habit. The certificate stands for a special training course which is competence-oriented, and we still think that recent evidence of learning in a mature student is the best evidence for hiring." Or as one of her associates bluntly adds: "We don't believe in all this labeling, credentialism and degrees, but if you can't lick them you join them—to a degree." The price that the Center may have to pay for accreditation could be a loss of autonomy to experiment. Credit for some types of experience, such as volunteer work or part-time jobs, makes sense to the staff, and the certificate program would be the most likely vehicle for such experimentation. But the certificate program can now be tied to the New School BA; and when it is, the program comes under the jurisdiction of other departments. According to Dean Allen Austill, the New School is not taking the initiative in pioneering credit for work experience. The Center, reflecting the interests of its clientele, is very interested in the idea of giving credit for life experiences. Ms. Van Doren thinks the issue will be raised piecemeal by each student making a special case to the dean. "That's the way change occurs in the academic world—slowly," she says.

The Center is expensive; an average certificate course costs $80; however, courses taken for New School credit cost $85 a credit. Ms. Van Doren is worried about the women who cannot afford the tuition and is looking for ways to reduce the cost. One way she suggests is through the College Board's College-Level Examination Program (CLEP). This national program offers a series of tests for which many colleges give credit to students who make suitable scores. Ms. Van Doren has asked the New School faculty to point out courses for which students may earn credit through CLEP tests. Ms. Van Doren encourages women to take one or two courses outside their homes to satisfy the need to "get out," and she suggests they form small "listening groups" with other women to view academic courses given on television.

Ms. Van Doren is concerned with widening the Center's constituency. "What can you do for the bright secretary who needs more education but can't get release time from her employer to improve her skills? We need scholarships as well as better counseling and vocational placement help. Without scholarship funds we shut the lower-income women out of the Center—and that will be our loss." The list of projects that Ms. Van Doren wants to undertake for the Center is long: "We should be opening up other training areas in the communications media, in the environmental field and in the paralegal and community-action fields. Why not women lobbyists or housing inspectors?" she says.

The insistent note of "me, me, me" Ruth Van Doren hears from her students signals a change of attitude to be reckoned with. To this observer it seemed as important as any of the overt activity occurring in the Center's classrooms. An unappealing refrain? Perhaps by traditional norms, but not when explained by two gray-haired women who were taking a course on self-awareness and the awareness of others. "I'm a widow and am more interested in the lives of my family than in my own. I want to get out of myself and out of my family." Three chairs away from her the same theme was echoed: "I come from a large family. My life's consisted of doing—doing for my family, then doing for my husband and doing for my children. Now I want to do for me."

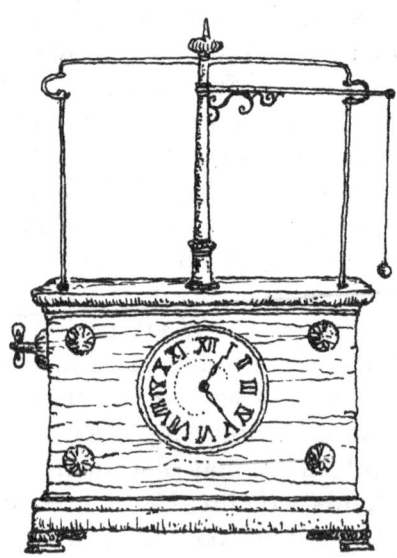

A Fair Return

By Diane Rothbard Margolis

Whatever became of the women of the Silent Generation, those coeds of the fifties who took lecture notes while knitting argyle socks for their boyfriends—and never dropped a stitch? Where are they now, the mothers of the baby boom, the settlers of the suburbs? What did they do when their bubble burst in the mid-sixties, when Betty Friedan told them what they'd already sensed: successful husbands, well-decorated "splits," and high-achieving children do not a full life make?

Some simply denounced Friedan and went back to their kitchens, taking up needlepoint to soothe their ruffles. Others found jobs or discovered ways to work some vocational partnership with their husbands—fulfilling a dream cherished among those housewives yet so secret even Friedan failed to detect it. Still others, like me, took Friedan's all-American, all-purpose cure—more education.

Now, along with approximately 410,000 other adult women, I am enrolled in an institution of higher education. It isn't possible to know whether I am part of a trend: until 1972 the Bureau of the Census didn't count those over 34 attending college. Perhaps the bureau's directors shared the bias of the chief secretary of the sociology department where I am registered, a woman heard to remark that enrollees over that age belong in another sort of institution. That worthy, no spring chicken herself, once opened an admissions application and whooped, "She must be crazy—what does a 40-year-old woman want to go to graduate school for?"

What for indeed! Everybody knows the appropriate place for such a woman is an adult education program. Such programs might enrich deficit-ridden institutions but are worthless to career aspirants. The courses tend to be jazzed up or watered down—"flower arranging" instead of "botany," "altered states of consciousness" instead of "psychology," and "folk music" rather than "musicology." True, in recent years a few colleges have developed regular degree programs for adults. But in the sixties if a woman desired a serious education she had to attend a conventional university. Even today if she seeks a graduate or professional degree, she has no choice but to matriculate in an alien institution, a place designed for the young. Thus by choosing seriousness, she risks the ridiculous.

The alumna of the fifties' panty raids walks into the classroom 20 years later with the dignity of a matron, the protected sensibilities of a housewife, and a sense of justice learned while protecting her young from the minor atrocities of elementary schools. She finds herself not among that community of scholars she anticipated but in a bureaucracy geared to instruct and dispatch adolescents. Professors are her own age, or, worse yet, not much older than her children. She doesn't know how to deal with them, nor they her. The usual relationship between student and professor—painfully hierarchical—requires a degree of student obsequiousness that the suburban housewife has long forgotten. At first she might be indignant at careless slights: professors forget appointments and lose papers; advisers vanish to other campuses. She might even fight for her "rights," as I did when I knocked at deans' doors with bitter complaints. But she soon learns that common courtesy in academia is as uncommon as middle-aged women, and after a year or two she reverts to childish attitudes, responding to affronts with "Oh, that's all right," and sometimes even meaning it.

When that happens her regression is complete. Mine is. I have been back at school for a decade. I am now an accomplished social chameleon, able to change my actions and expectations as frequently as I switch roles from suburban princess to student vassal and from self-assured local politician to faltering acolyte in political sociology. But there was a time when I confused the roles, when my personality was integrated and my behavior absurd.

That was my first year back at school. I once argued for half a class period that an exam based on material which had been covered scantily in the text and not at all in the lectures was unfair. My young classmates supported me until the professor agreed to curve the grades. The adjustment having been made, nobody understood why I continued to press the point. There was, I thought, some basic principle which needed defense—I can't remember it now.

On another occasion I went to complain to a department head about an instructor who read his lectures from an alternate text. Was that not a form of plagiarism? Didn't academic excellence require a different approach? After listening between telephone calls, the chairman suggested that I adjust to the situation. I did, and took a giant step that day toward appropriate studenthood. I bought the alternate text and began cutting classes.

By the time I ran into Professor X, I had given up quibbling and my reformation seemed complete. I listened in silence to his impassioned harangues against "garbage"—blacks, Puerto Ricans, Communists, Vietnamese, and women. I marveled quietly at his exquisite device for student control: regular quizzes based on the first and last sentences of the paragraphs or footnotes in the assigned text; he read the first half of the sentences, and we had to deliver the second half verbatim. By midterm most of the class was failing and dependent on his benevolence. But not I. I was stoically memorizing one hundred sentences a night. What finally made me revert to activism was not his quizzes but his sense of humor. Too often the butt of his dirty jokes was one or another young coed who would run blushing or weeping from the room.

The victims reawakened my motherly sensibilities. So, seeking only to have his courses removed from the degree requirements, I presented written notes on X's classroom antics to the dean. Those notes became the dean's evidence for a dismissal he had long desired. Thus, by the end of the semester my peculiarities had combined with X's to give him early retirement and me lasting notoriety. I was graduated from that school seven years ago, but on my rare visits back I'm introduced as "the one who got rid of X." I'm not pleased. I had not, after all, returned to school to purge the university. Nor does such repute sit easily on the conscience of one raised in a time when women were taught to be seen and not heard.

A year after the Professor X affair I went on to graduate school. There I felt misplaced as much for my sex as for my age. Women of my generation rarely attempted doctorates. Or to be more accurate, only 7,598 women (compared with

69,529 men) earned their doctorates during the entire decade of the fifties. And I did not know any of them. Friends who went to women's colleges respond to my envy over the role models they had in the form of female professors by describing the eccentricities of those learned but lonely ladies. The stories suggest they were a little like Roberta, my college dormmate in the fifties, who went on to medical school. She wore blue fingernail polish.

It was, I suppose, her way of marking herself off from the rest of us who dreamed of doctors, not doctorates. And the choice had to be made; few women could have both. Now, as I attempt a career without forsaking the joys of family life, without making myself in some way unlovable, I have an odd feeling that somehow I'm an impostor, that I don't belong. Perhaps that is one reason that, like so many overage students, I cram for each examination as if my life depended on it. That's why I and others who at 18 could accept a breezy "C" with equanimity return to school as insufferable grinds.

We overwork, overworry, and overbear to the annoyance of our husbands and younger fellow students. One woman I know went so far as to take her textbooks to bed with her; feeling crowded, her husband soon left. Another, when she received a grade less than "A," which was seldom enough, would set up meetings with her professor to *explain*—as if it mattered to him. It *does* matter to us. We are trying to catch up with male cohorts whose careers took a speedier, more direct line. The shift in our life's direction that marks our return is not a new flexibility—it is a last chance.

Fearful of losing another minute or of making another mistake, we study compulsively. We treat each grade as the ultimate measure of our worth. For we are back in college because housewife-mother was a status so unsatisfactory we are willing to be treated like children again in order some day to have a job that lets us do honorable work. To get a "C," and for some even a "B," would create an unbearable sense of failure. So we memorize 100 sentences each night if that is what an "A" seems to require. We write 30-page papers when 12 pages would do. Often we score 10 points above everyone else.

No wonder our fellow students sometimes become irritated. And, as if our skewing class curves were not enough, some of us dominate classroom discussions with the experiences of our years—trying perhaps to catch the professor's notice, to share something with the only age-mate around. College is a lonely place for those who have no peers.

Occasionally over the past decade I have spotted another sagging chin across the classroom. We talk for a while, only to discover that she lives in New Jersey and I in Connecticut. After class we go back home to our housekeeping and our mothering. For us role change or liberation is a slow process, and old tasks do not end when studying begins. We have not returned to school to find friends. We have returned to do what was unthinkable in the fifties—to launch a career.

Perhaps we chose the easiest and most cowardly launching pad. If we attempted to escape from our doll's house by joining institutions for juveniles, who was to complain? We didn't abandon our kitchens and children for full-time employment. Instead we took one or two courses a semester; our way was slow and gentle, hardly noticeable.

Last May, on parents' day, my husband and I visited our son at college. We lunched in the dining hall, toured the library and the student union, helped dedicate a new music building, and took Harry and his roommate out to dinner. As we were leaving, walking down the path between the lilac and magnolia, ducking frisbees, I had a thought. "Harry," I asked, "you haven't shown us any classrooms—this is a school, isn't it?"

"Oh! They're over there," he said, pointing vaguely to a remote part of campus. "They're not really that important; I only spend 12 hours a week in class."

I knew then that I had never really returned to college: I had only nipped off a small portion of that experience. We send our young off to college not only to imbibe heady masses of our accumulated knowledge and technique but to learn to live independently with their peers. I and those other peerless matrons have gotten only half a loaf. Our sisters who eschewed the scholarly route and went straight to work at whatever job they could get without credentials got the other, and maybe the better, half.

I think of my friends: Joan who went to work parttime for a local weekly and is now a star reporter—at least on the prison beat; Martha who 10 years ago began as a publisher's secretary and is now full-time publicity director of a major publishing house; Sandy who started as a receptionist in a real estate office and now outsells most of the men there. They have experience; they have careers. And they have been working alongside men their own age all the years while I and others who went back to school have delayed the moment when we would storm those male bastions—the elite professions.

Oh well! Education always has been a matter of delayed pleasures. But why didn't we know, why didn't Friedan tell us, that we might be taking too long? That we would be applying for our first jobs when men our age were preparing for their retirements. That by the seventies a PhD would be another drug on the market, a passport to a vanishing country.

Now, as I prepare my dissertation, I keep wondering: Did it make sense to memorize all those footnotes? Did I grow in some way I still don't understand when I learned to be grateful to professors who remembered to apologize for broken appointments? Was the game worth the candle?

Maybe. I have been teaching part-time for a while, and a friend who came to my class as a guest lecturer said later that seeing me in front of my students he thought of me for the first time as a *person*—not as a mere adjunct to my husband. That's progress!

As Lady Mary Wortley Montague remarked on her deathbed, "It has all been very interesting." Returning to school may or may not be the way to stay young—a questionable goal in any case—but it is surely not the way to grow old gracefully.